The Online Classroom

Written by Eileen Giuffré Cotton

Produced by the staff of
Classroom Connect,
creators of premier Internet
products for K – 12 educators

classroom
CONNECT

2221 Rosecrans Avenue
El Segundo, CA 90245
URL: http://www.classroom.com
Email: connect@classroom.com
(8 0 0) 6 3 8 - 1 6 3 9

W9-CQY-080

To Chet
my husband
and
Eustace, Helen, and Leo Giuffré
my uncle, mother, and father

classroom
CONNECT®

Senior Editor: Kathleen Housley
Design and Illustration: Jay Walters
Contributing Writers: Tim Dougherty, Dave Kershaw
Editor: Dorissa Bolinski

About the Author

Eileen Giuffre Cotton is a world-wide teacher. She has taught in public schools in California, at the University of Guam, and is currently a professor of education at California State University, Chico. Her travels have taken her to every state in the U.S. and extensively in Canada, as well as the British Isles, the Orient, and Down Under. Her summers are spent in Wyoming with Chet, her husband for 25 years, on their mountainside, where she wrote *The Online Classroom*. She collects teddy bears, drives a diesel pickup truck, likes RVs and steam engines, and recently bought her sixth computer.

Dr. Cotton's scholarly articles are in print throughout the professional literature, but you are more likely to encounter her making a presentation at a conference — she likes to work with teachers. *The Online Classroom* is also an online course:

URL: http://www.indiana.edu/
~eric_rec/disted/internet/
530form.html

A book is the work of many people, not just the author.
Specifically, I want to thank all the K-12 teachers who gave me ideas for lessons, the folks at ERIC/REC for their time, energy, and patience, and my friends and colleagues for all the encouragement they gave me.

Thank you one and all.

Forward

Classrooms without doors

A popular phrase coined by young race car enthusiasts is "blow the doors off", meaning to take advantage of, or go to the extreme, to win in a competition. But this superlative isn't limited to racing cars. If a particular person, place or thing can "blow the doors off", the speaker believes there is none other that is better, faster or more desirable.

Would your students say the same about you, or your classroom? There's a good chance they will, as you begin to utilize the power and excitement of the Internet in your classroom. The simple fact that you are reading this means you are about to join the ranks of over a million teachers in more than 160 countries who have already discovered the wealth of resources on the Internet. And we aren't just talking about online repositories of texts and databases that seemed so interesting a few years ago.

How is the Internet being used in the classroom? Teachers and students are making new friends and studying cultures around the world through email exchanges and collaborative learning projects; amazing and free Cu-See-Me software allows students to participate in global – and local – video conferencing; electronic field trips provide dozens of exciting opportunities to "visit" zoos, museums, underwater explorations and far away archaeological digs; "ask-an-expert" allows anyone, anywhere to communicate with more than ninety topic-specific experts in over eleven countries. All of this, and much more, is happening everyday in classrooms around the world. Students are becoming more enthusiastic about learning, and are building knowledge in new ways, using the Internet.

This book will show you how to do all of this and more. It's not hard – this book makes it easy. It will take a little time and effort on your part, but it will be worth it many times over. You'll energize your existing lesson plans, and make learning – and teaching – more fun and exciting than ever.

So, gentle reader, get started! Learn the basics of the Internet and you'll soon amaze your peers and students. With a little effort and creativity, you can open up unlimited opportunities for your students. Try it. You'll soon "blow the doors off" your classroom.

Gregory Giagnocavo
Director, Classroom Connect
jgg@classroom.net

P.S. We'd love to hear how you're using the Internet in the classroom.
If you have experiences or ideas you'd like to share with other teachers, please email them to me at **jgg@classroom.net** and we'll pass them on.

Table of Contents

Dedication

About the Author

Acknowledgments

Preface

Table of Contents

Section I: The Mechanics

Chapter 1
Introduction to the Internet 1-8

Chapter 2
The World Wide Web 9-22

Chapter 3
A Wealth of Web Sites 23-54

Chapter 4
Searching on the Web 55-66

Chapter 5
Developing and Designing a Web Page 67-88

Chapter 6
Advanced Web 89-102

Chapter 7
The Other Internet Tools .103-122

Section II: Lesson Plans and Other Ways to Use the Internet

Chapter 8
E-pals and Keypals 123-136

Chapter 9
A Whale of a Time 137-146

Chapter 10
The News 147-158

Chapter 11
Look Who's Talking! 159-172

Chapter 12
Virtually Together in D.C. 173-184

Chapter 13
The Games People Play 185-194

Chapter 14
The ABCs of the Internet 195-206

Chapter 15
Get a Job! 207-212

Chapter 16
A Book an Hour .213-220

Chapter 17
Just for the Little Kids 221-232

Appendix A
Bibliography 233-236

Appendix B
Glossary 237-245

Appendix C
The Online Classroom CD-ROM 246-247

Chapter 1

Introduction to the Internet

The Internet first entered my life when I saw an advertisement for 10 free hours of America Online (AOL). I sent away for the program, and as soon as I loaded it onto my computer, set up my modem, and logged on, I was hooked.

I like to push buttons and play with gadgets, so cruising AOL was a logical extension of a natural bent. I visited all the different departments available, and quickly ran out of free time. There was so much to do and so little time to do it!

The next autumn, my university provided all faculty members with an email account and access to the Internet via Mosaic, TurboGopher, Fetch, and telnet. Being a pro who had already used AOL, I set out to explore some more.

I visited lots of sites and decided again that this Internet stuff held great potential for my students. Unfortunately, I kept running out of time to learn more. Then came winter break when I was able to spend 3,000 minutes on the Internet. I explored, learned, crashed into virtual walls, and survived the crashes. I became convinced that the Internet was a place to learn while having a good time. I could tune in and turn on my students.

The learning was fascinating and interesting, and NOW! Perseverance had paid off. I wanted more out of the Net. I wanted to set up home pages, get my students connected, develop lists and links and lessons, play some games, and just surf. All my surfing and crashing led eventually to this book. The Internet: I love it, and — I hope — so will you and your students.

I am not a computer expert, techie, or digit-head. I know some buzz words, but I do not babble in technospeak. I know how to use the word processing, spreadsheet, database, and draw programs. Thanks to the Internet, I know how to download programs and files, too. Don't fear. The only skill you really need to be successful on the Internet is the ability to use a keyboard and follow directions.

There is one other thing you need, *time*. It takes time to find Web sites on the Internet and to develop lessons that will be useful and meaningful to your students. That's why I wrote this book. I want to make your introduction to the Internet smooth and easy. With this book, you won't lose time aimlessly wandering around the Net. You can be up and on the Net in no time.

Before long, you'll be integrating the Internet into your style of teaching. To help you get started, I've included ideas that you can use in your classroom. You can begin using these lessons immediately. All the Web sites and their addresses have been tested. I promise you: Give the Internet a chance, and your kids will learn from it.

Organization of *The Online Classroom*

This book is divided into two sections: The Mechanics; and Lesson Plans and Other Ways to Use the Internet. Both sections talk about programs and components of the Internet. In the Mechanics section, you'll learn about how to navigate the Internet and use all the Net tools. The second section contains lessons with clearly stated goals, rationales, objectives, procedures, and evaluation guidelines. Unlike other books on the Internet that start with the history of each type of navigation program, this book starts with the easiest things to do on the Internet and progresses from there. As you progress through the book and become more confident in what you can do, the lessons become more challenging.

Included in each chapter are teacher resources or lessons that you can use now. To make the lessons teacher friendly, I have provided all the Web sites or links you will need. You'll notice that some of the lessons can be finished in a single day, while some are units of instruction that will take from two to five weeks (or more) to complete.

In the lesson plans, I have purposely not stated exact grade levels. Each lesson is designed so that you can easily adapt it to fit your specific classroom needs. You can make each lesson easier or more difficult, depending on the ability of your students. Keep in mind that when the kids are learning something new, they do not seem to mind material that might appear too simple. However, once they have learned a functional Internet process or technique, students will automatically find their individual levels of use.

All of the lessons encourage small-group work. Sitting in front of a computer by yourself can be lonely. Working with a classmate is not only more interesting and more fun, but doubles your troubleshooting and problem-solving power. It becomes easier to figure out why the computer is not behaving as expected or where to search for some elusive topic of interest. The Internet encourages connections among ideas, so that when two or three students work together at a computer, the potential for connectivity increases proportionally. These pages, therefore, do not contain quiet-corner lessons. These lessons will stir up the noise of learning. This is good. Your job is to encourage the positive noise and discourage the negative, meanwhile monitoring the process to make sure that your students stay on task. Finally, as peer collaboration is good for students, so it is for teachers. Use this book and explore teaching with the Internet in company with a fellow teacher and you will enjoy, and benefit from, both the book and the Net. In addition, if you can learn using this book on the Internet with a fellow teacher, you will enjoy both the book and the Internet more, too.

Once you have grasped the basics of how the Internet can serve you as a teacher, you will be traveling the Web to explore your own interests. You will discover the wealth of information out there that you would never have imagined was so readily available. You may also reinvent your entire approach to teaching and learning. All of that is up to you. The Internet can make you a teacher in an "online classroom" anywhere in the world.

What you need to access the Internet

I hope I've whetted your appetite for using the Internet and teaching with the wealth of information it has to enrich your class. If so, here is what you need: curiosity, a personal computer of some sort (either Macintosh or IBM-type PC), a high-speed modem, a telephone line, and appropriate software for a graphical connection. The computer, modem, and telephone line are relatively easy to get; the connection software may be a bit more difficult. I've also written this book for graphical-type computers; that means, a Macintosh computer (which I do have) or a PC with Windows 3.1 or Windows 95. The examples that I give will come from a Macintosh Power PC 7200, but that really does not matter. The Internet is not computer-specific. That means, most of the screens will look similar whether on a Mac or PC. So if a window, screen, or picture shown in this book does not exactly match the window, screen, or picture on your computer, don't worry, you should notice some similarity. The bottom line is, we will probably be able to do the same thing, even if we don't get there in exactly the same way. That means you just have to point and click (and occasionally type) to get where you need to go.

It depends on where you live in the U.S. as to what type of Internet access is available to you at the price you are willing to pay. Some cities and towns have access through a school district, county office of education, the state department of education, the local telephone company, or local businesses. Probably the ideal situation for a teacher is to have school-system-wide Internet access and a savvy technician at your elbow to answer all your questions and make the computer work. I have that type of access in California through my university. Failing that, many commercial Internet providers are in business to supply you with the software needed to access the Internet.

There are local and national commercial Internet providers. Some of the most readily available national providers are America OnLine (AOL), CompuServe, WOW, ATT, Prodigy, GEnie, MicroSoft Internet Connection in

Win 95, and NetCom. In the appendix there is a comparison of national Internet providers. Several regional telephone companies provide Internet access, as well as many local Internet providers. If you look in the Yellow Pages of the telephone book under "Internet" you will see many listings. In some states and areas, there are regional networks—some of them free called "freenets," some of them inexpensive — accessible by means of a local telephone call and hence available to teachers and schools and the public. On the downside, some places in the U.S. do not yet have this capability, but they should be getting access soon. I was going to list all the access providers out there, but the Internet is growing and the technology is changing so rapidly that my list would be quickly out of date.

The computer in my office at school is hard wired into the campus **server** — that way I do not need to use my telephone line. To get on the Internet, I merely turn on my computer, click on the program icon I want, and I'm there in the blink of an eye. At home, I access that same server over the telephone lines using a 14.4 modem and a dial-up Internet access program called ARA (Area Remote Access). When I'm on the Internet at home, my phone line is busy.

To gain Internet access to write this book, I took my Mac and modem with me to Etna, Wyoming. Using MacPPP (Point to Point Protocol dial-up Internet access program) I dialed into a local server called CyberHighway.Net out of Boise, Idaho. When I give a presentation somewhere away from my campus, I use another server called Telis which gives me free 800 service anywhere in California. This means I have three email accounts, with three different email addresses. But no matter where I am, I have access to the Internet — and I'm at the center of the universe of information and communication.

For practical purposes, you don't really need to know about the type of server that you have access to or the type of connection required or most of the other technical jargon and specs (that's what techies are for!). What you do need to know is that the Internet is there and accessible. It's mostly user friendly (and getting better all the time), and it's definitely filled with information that you can use in your classroom to make lessons more exciting and real for your students.

Censorship?

The bad stuff: The Internet is a human invention, put together by computer savvy adults for their own various reasons. Some things on the Internet are not appropriate for everyone. Some things are questionable, some things are highly inappropriate, and some things on the Internet are just downright bad for children (and adults, too)! You can be sure that your students will find the good, the bad, and the ugly. Filtered among the Web sites you will see x-rated material, advocacy of violence, invitations to buy things that are prohibited to underage people, inappropriate invitations via email to write to people who might have perverted intentions, invitations to purchase items with credit cards, etc. Don't let this get you down. There is not as much as the "nay sayers" say there is, and there is far more good stuff on the Internet.

Depending on what you read these days, there are "tons of smut" on the net, and there is no way to protect yourself or your kids — whether your own children or your students — from it. But the truth is the good outweighs the evil on the Internet, and there are means of protecting ourselves against objectionable Web sites. Most national Internet providers offer some type of screening program for parents or teachers to filter out the negative Web sites. America OnLine, for example, offers a "Protection Program." In addition, you can purchase one of several screening programs, if you feel it is needed. In my nearly five years of random surfing on the Internet, I must say that I have not encountered many objectionable Web sites. There are, however, some sexually explicit sites and questionable or objectionable Web sites on the Internet. When I see one, I ignore it. Kids won't. To that end, I tell my students some "rules of the road" that must be followed. In classrooms where teachers use the Internet all the time, they tell their students not to visit these Web sites, and then they regularly monitor their students' use of the computers. We do not want to stop all access to the Internet just because a few Web sites are questionable. It is part of our job as educators to teach young people how to cope with the unhappy realities of life. I believe that teachers and parents need to tell their kids what they should and should not do and then make the consequences of violating the rules fit the crime. That's discipline. That's education.

As a teacher, you can do a lot to help kids cope with the bad stuff in their world, including the bad stuff that assails them on the Net. One of your jobs is to encourage your students to stay on the right track. Another of your jobs is to be forthright with them in discussing the dangers that lurk, have always lurked, and shall forever lurk out there in reality. I've asked a lot of teachers and parents what they say to their kids. The following speech is more or less the essence of what most people say:

> "There's good and bad on the Internet. I give you free access to the good, but I ask you to respect your fellow classmates and me and stay away from the questionable side of the Net. Please do not let me catch you surfing to restricted sites, as I will be forced to take action that will be less than pleasing to you. If you do not understand why pornography, violence, and other abuses are bad for you, stop by my desk after class and let's talk it over."

If your lessons are well planned, tight and packed with information, you'll be most able to keep your kids out of trouble. To ensure that will happen, you might want to develop an Acceptable Use Policy for your classroom, school, or district. An Acceptable Use Policy (AUP) is an agreement among teachers, students, parents, and school officials that outlines the rules that will be followed by everyone who has access to the Internet. Most schools have or are developing AUPs to maintain an orderly and effective use of the Internet. In Chapter 3, I discuss AUPs and offer some Web sites where you can read other AUPs to find ideas for writing one that will meet your needs or the needs of your school or district.

Now you're ready!

There is yet another problem — the problem of time. The Internet is sometimes hard to leave. There is so much information out there, and you'll want to see it all. Surfing the Web, cataloguing information, making connections, thinking, and making connections are very addicting pastimes. I haven't solved this problem myself, but I do have a little advice. People often say to me, "There is so much information out there, how do you know where to start, or stop for that matter?"

I respond that when you go to the library, you don't walk in and say, "There are so many books, I want to read them all." Instead you may browse for a while and wish to read lots, but eventually you settle on just a few books to take home. You must treat the Internet the same. There is a lot of information out there, but after looking around for a while, you need to start honing in on what it is you want to find, and then set a limit on how much time you can spend online. Otherwise you can fall in and never come out.

Anyway, that's enough for now. There is so much more to know, but you won't get anywhere until you start using the Internet to help you out in the classroom. Thus, to learn to surf this ocean of information, you need to get wet. Let's go surfing.

Chapter 2

The World Wide Web

In Internet books published as late as 1994, the wonders of gopher and telnet are lauded. If you read these books, you can learn how to access GopherSpace and ftp archives. If you keep reading them, however, you will probably become confused. These programs are still used (see Chapter 7), but they are not as user friendly as a generic World Wide Web (WWW) browser. Thank goodness times have changed! Thank goodness for multipurpose browsers!

In this chapter we plunge into the World Wide Web using one of the easiest navigation programs around: Netscape Navigator or "Netscape." But first, let me explain how the Internet works by giving you the big picture. I'll try not to be too technical, but feel free to skip over the next couple of paragraphs if you are not interested in how the Internet connects us all.

The Internet is a global network of computers connected through communication links, such as ordinary phone lines. Some computers connected to the Internet, called "servers," store information that can be retrieved from other computers, called "clients." When you use your computer to retrieve information from the Internet, your computer is acting as a client, and it is getting information from a server, through the connections on the global network.

The World Wide Web consists of servers and clients on the Internet that communicate using a standard language. Using the same language allows different kinds of servers and clients to communicate with each other, even if they are made by different manufacturers. This language allows your computer (a client) to retrieve text, pictures, sounds, and animation from any server, via the Internet. However, to retrieve that information, you need a Web browser.

There are many Web browsers out there . . . Cello, Mosaic, Lynx, Netscape, Quarterdeck, and Internet Explorer, among others. They all fall into two main categories: text based and graphics based. A text-based browser allows you to see just the words, whereas a graphics-based browser lets you experience images, sounds, and even animation.

The first browser I used was Mosaic. Mosaic was marvelous, if a little slow. Then I found out that I could download — for free — a wonderful program called Netscape. So, I downloaded Netscape and gave it a spin. I never went back to Mosaic. I've downloaded various updates of the original Netscape (Versions 1.1, 2.0, 2.02, 3.0). Just recently, I downloaded another browser, Microsoft's Internet Explorer for the Macintosh — one of the newer browsers available.

That is a great example of how fast things change! Netscape and Internet Explorer are the best browsers available right now. Tomorrow or next week, someone else will develop a better browser, with faster download times, more built-in multimedia, and bells and whistles. Until then, I'll stick with Netscape and Internet Explorer as I browse the Web. Only as a last resort do I use gopher and ftp navigation programs.

The Internet and ways to navigate it are changing every day. To be a successful surfer on the Web, you need to be flexible. If you're not flexible, you can easily become tangled in a spider web of information.

Netscape does cost money. The good news is that if you are a teacher, you can download it for free.

URL: http://www.netscape.com

You can also download Internet Explorer from the Microsoft Web site.

URL: http://microsoft.com

Once at either site, you will need to indicate the type of computer (Macintosh, Windows, DOS, UNIX) you have, click on the correct link, and wait while it downloads. Both of these Web sites are busy, so the companies have provided mirror sites with the same programs. These programs are easy to download but they may take a few minutes because of their size! If you're too intimidated to download a program, you can probably acquire the most recent version of Netscape or Internet Explorer from your computer techie.

Browsers

Look at the picture of the Netscape screen below, and let's play with the buttons to find out what they do. If your computer and your browser are different from mine — and they probably are — don't worry, as you will see they are similar enough. Each version (Macintosh, Windows, DOS, UNIX) is a little different, so be patient, be flexible, and translate what I am saying into the bells and whistles on the screen right before your face. Netscape relies on these buttons and pull-down menus as the easy-to-operate controls of the program. You need not memorize them — it all comes with practice.

Tool Bar Buttons

The first row of square buttons is called the "tool bar display," and the first button you see is *Back*. If the *Back* button is faint, then it is not yet activated — because you have not yet gone anywhere, there's no "back" for *Back* to go to. As you surf along, *Back* will become darker; now you can click on *Back* to go back to wherever you were before, one step at a time, until you finally come to where you started.

Click on *Forward* and it takes you — guess where? — forward along the path you have been traveling. This way you can move back and forth, revisiting sites without losing your way or having to key in long URL strings.

Home will take you all the way back to the opening Web page where you started. The default home page for Netscape is the Netscape Web site, but you can change that by going into *Options*. I recommend that you change it, because when everyone has their browser programmed to the same default home page, you will experience a long wait time to get started. I'll explain a trick on setting your home page in the section on preferences.

Click on *Reload* when you are working with real-time graphics and when Netscape bogs down and seems to need refreshing. *Reload* will give you a new image. At some Web sites you can click on *Reload* every few minutes to reveal a new picture.

Images will turn on the graphics (if you have them off). I usually turn the *auto load images* function off if I am working on a modem. If I'm working on a dedicated line (in my office) I turn the *images* on. Because *images* take a long time to load and you can always click an individual image on if you want to see it, it is a time and patience-saving device. Also, if you have a slower computer, you can turn off the *auto load image* feature.

Open allows you to move to a new Web site. A dialogue box will appear where you type the Web site address or URL (Universal Resource Locator) you want to go to. Key *Return* or *OK*, and your browser will take you there.

Print prints the page. *Find* will help you locate something quickly on the Web page that you are reading. This button will do a keyword search.

Stop can be one of the greatest buttons around. Sometimes your browser just doesn't feel well that day, and it grinds and grinds, and shall grind forever, trying to load a document. Click on *Stop* and give it a rest! Then, when you start over, it may load like a charm (and they call this scientific!). *Stop* is a great time-saver; one that I use a lot. Most browsers have a *Stop* function! Thank goodness, as waiting is something that I am not good at doing.

The *Go To* or *Location* box is located under the tool bar. This box displays either the field where you type the URL of your next destination or it displays the URL where you are right now.

Directory Buttons

Directory Buttons make up the third row, and they are for surfing fun. Click on *What's New?* to see some of the hundreds of new Web sites that appear each week. *What's Cool?* presents a list of potentially fun and interesting Web sites for that week. In a Netscape browser, *Handbook* will transport you to a great tutorial on how to use Netscape. This one's a biggie. Since I'm not covering every aspect of Netscape, *Handbook* will fill in all the details I'm leaving out. *Net Search* or *Net Directory* provides you with a list of search engines and directories for the World Wide Web. These buttons give you the capability to search the Web, either by key word or by category. The last button is *Software*. Click on it to discover the latest software available from the Netscape folks.

If you have a small screen, the tool bar buttons and directory buttons can be closed. Many of the features they offer are also available in the pull-down menus, which I'll talk about next.

Pull-down menus

File
- New Web Browser
- New Mail Message
- Mail Document...
- Open Location...
- Open File...

- Close
- Save as...
- Upload File...

- Page Setup...
- Print...

- Quit

Pull down *File* and scroll down *New Browser*, *New Mail Message*, *Open Location*, and *Open File*. *Open Location* is the same as the open button. *Open File* means it will open an HTML file from your hard drive or diskette. *Open File* is used a lot when you are creating HTML documents, as this is how you check them for accuracy. *File* is also the location of *Page Setuip* and *Quit*. Always know how to quit a program!

Pull down *Edit* and you see the usual cut, copy, paste, and clear commands you find on most word processing programs. There is also a *Select All* option that let's you block a whole Web page. I use the *Edit* commands when I'm using my browser and a word processing program, blocking, copying, and pasting from the browser to the word processing program.

Edit
- Undo
- Cut
- Copy
- Paste
- Clear
- Select All
- Find...
- Find Again

Pull down *View* and scroll to *Document Source* to see that Web page written in HTML source codes. In chapter 5 you will learn more about HTML. Pull down *Go*, and you are greeted with a history of the titles of every site where you have been during your current Web session. Pull down *Go*

View
- Reload
- Reload Frame
- Load Images
- Document Source
- Document Info
- Frame Source
- Frame Info

and click on the title of any document, home page, or link to which you would like to return directly (as opposed to going *Back* one step at a time). Pull down *Bookmarks*, click on *Add Bookmark*, and voila, whatever URL is current on your screen will be added permanently to your bookmark collection — yours forever until you delete it. (URLs in *Go* are not saved; when you turn Netscape off,

Bookmarks
- Add Bookmark
- Favorite Places
- K-12 Education Sites
- Science Sites
- Interesting site #1
- Interesting site #2
- Interesting site #3
- Interesting site #4
- Interesting site #5
- Interesting site #6

everything in *Go* will be gone.) *Bookmarks* is as nifty a time saver as *Stop*. As you explore the Web, you will find sites to which you will want to return again and again. *Bookmarks* allows you to save your favorite URLs for quick and easy access. My bookmark collection is humongous, and with the newer browsers it is really easy to organize. Just mouse over

to *Window* and scroll to *Bookmarks*. Click on it and you will see your list of bookmarks that you can organize into folders and then sort in alphabetical order if you want. By the way, if you are using Internet Explorer, *Favorites* is the same as *Bookmarks*.

Pull down *Options* to set up Netscape to suit yourself. You set *Preferences* for the general display, mail and news, network, and security. You can turn off and on *Auto Load Images*, the *Directory Buttons*, the *Tool Bar*, and the *Go To* locations. Just remember, every time you make a change to something in *Options*, you must save it. If you do not save it, then Netscape will not remember what you told it to do the next time you turn it on. Depending on which version of Netscape you are running, you will see slightly different iterations of this pull-down menu. When in doubt, click on *Handbook* and get the correct configuration for your version.

Options
General Preferences...
Mail and News Preferences...
Network Preferences...
Security Preferences...
Show Toolbar
Show Location
Show Directory Buttons
Show Java Console
Auto Load Images
Document Encoding

Remember that trick I told you about changing your home page? This is where you do it. Pull down *Options* and scroll to *General Preferences*. A window will appear showing a set of files. Click on the *Appearance* file. The screen is divided into three sections: *Toolbar*, *Startup*, and *Link Styles*. Look in *Startup* and you will see a prompt that says "Browser starts with" then "blank page" or "home page location" and a box. In that box, type the home page you would like to see every time you start your browser. I set my husband's browser to show my picture every time he starts up so he won't forget who I am.

Opening your first Web page

"Half the fun of going is getting there," say the tourist agencies. Now that you know how to have fun getting there, where are you going to go? With your browser, you can navigate to any place in Cyberspace and tap into a wealth of knowledge.

Let's surf over to a famous address to discover what Web pages are like — 1600 Pennsylvania Avenue, Washington, D.C., the White House. In a browser, however, the address is called a URL for Universal Resource Locator (frequently pronounced "earl"). Click on *Open*, and when the dialogue box appears, type in http://www.whitehouse.gov/

In a few seconds, you will see a picture of the White House — you're in! (No security checks, no waiting in line; This is access!) After the greeting and the picture of the White House (both change according to the time of day), scroll to the 10 buttons: *President and Vice President*, *Interactive Citizen's Handbook*, *Virtual Library*, *Help Desk*, *What's New*, *White House History and Tours*, *Briefing Room*, *Site News*, *Federal Services*, and *White House for Kids*. Click on any of these buttons and be treated to what's happening right now in the White House.

I especially like the *History and Tours* button as it gives a brief bio on each of the presidents and first ladies, but the *White House for Kids* button is a lot of fun, too. Click away on the different buttons and see what you get. Click on any of the links, and away you go — *Forward* and *Back* — click and surf. You've got the idea! Cool!

Scroll down that page and you will see words and images <u>underlined</u> (if you have a black and white monitor) or written in a different color (if you have a color monitor). Click on these underlined/colored links and you will automatically be transported to a related Web site. The first time I did this, I was already thinking: "This home page is going to make a great lesson for my class!"

By pointing and clicking in your browser, you have already become a Netsurfer. You can point and click and link your way to thousands of home pages and because about 1,200 are being added each week you have unlimited opportunities for finding great teaching materials.

Try another Web site. Click on *Open* and type in this

URL: http://www.ceismc.gatech.edu/BusyT/

It's the Busy Teachers' Web site home page.
Here you will find links to Archaeology,
Art, Astronomy, Biology, Chemistry,
Computer Technology, Ecology/
Environment, Elementary School,
English, Geology, High School Guidance
and Counseling, History, Mathematics,
Paleontology, Physics, Recess, Sciences
(Other), Social Studies, and a Teachers'

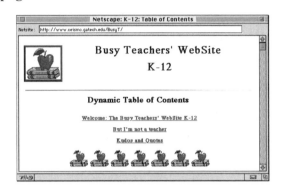

Reference Section. Carolyn Cole, who designed this Web site, wanted to provide
teachers with an easy-to-use source for materials, lesson plans, and classroom
activities. This Web site is easy to understand, so it is great for the Internet
beginner, and a time saver for the Internet pro.

Here are two other sites for you to browse to:

NetPets

URL: http://www.netpets.com/dogbreed.html

Godiva Chocolates

URL: http://www.godiva.com/

You have just typed in a few complicated URLs and you may be wondering
why they have to be so long and complex. With 1,200 new Web sites being added
each week and each one needing a unique URL, they have to be long so they can
be different. Once you know how to decode the letters and numbers of URLs,
however, URLs become a little easier to cope with and remember. Let's decode the
URL for the White House: http://www.whitehouse.gov/

http:// means it's a HyperText document
www means it appears on the World Wide Web

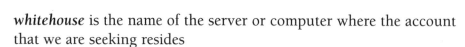

whitehouse is the name of the server or computer where the account that we are seeking resides

.gov means that the domain of the server is the government

All documents on the Web are written in something called HTML (HyperText Markup Language). HTML has underlined or colored words and phrases called hypertext links or links for short. These links allow you to move from one location to another at the click of your mouse. Therefore, a http document is one that is written in HTML and has links to other pages on the Web. This is useful to know as it means you do not need to know how to do anything else other than type in http:// (and in some browsers you don't even need to type this — a nice time saver as I get tired of typing colons and slashes all the time).

Every piece of information on the Internet is on a computer somewhere in the world and every computer has a name. That name is called a server or host. The name of the computer for the White House is called "whitehouse."

Finally there is the domain of the server. There are several different domains, all of which are represented with a dot and three letters, such as *.gov* or *.edu*. "Dot g-o-v" stands for government and sure enough, the White House is part of the government. Other domains include *.edu* for higher education Web sites; *.com* for commercial; *.k12* for k-12 education; *.org* for nonprofit organization; *.net* for network; and *.mil* for military. Sometimes if I know how to decode a URL I can determine if it is a reliable source of information. For example, I might rely on the information from a Web site developed by the government more than if it was developed by a commercial operation. This will make more sense as you surf the Web. Honest!

What to do when you don't get to where you want to go

Sometimes when you are browsing the Web, you are met by one of a dismaying array of negative responses. Chief among these are "403 Forbidden," "404 Not Found," and "Unable to connect to host."

Wow! How can something be "forbidden?" In you get that warning, that means that need to have a subscription or membership to access the site. Sometimes these may be free sites and sometimes you may have to pay, but in either case you will need to register for the site in order to get there. After you register, you will be given a password (which you must remember) to access the Web site again. No password, no go.

The "not found" message may indicate that the targeted Web site has moved to another location, has changed its name and URL, has just disappeared, or your Internet provider cannot find the location. When you get this message, try again in a little while, and it might be found. If it still is not found, then you might have to use a search engine and find the new URL, if it exists.

"Unable to connect" means the Web site is probably busy. If you try at another time, you might be able to connect. When school is first starting and all the kids are back on campus, I get the "unable to connect" message a lot because all the lines are busy! Once school has been in session about a month, I don't get the message any more.

Sometimes you may have trouble getting a URL to work. You may get another of those messages, "Code Not Found." If so, truncate the address — don't type the whole thing, back up a segment at a time from the right-hand side — and try it again. Sometimes nothing seems to work, your computer seems to be getting clogged up, everything's down, and your browser just cranks and cranks away, but goes nowhere. That's when it's time to pull the plug. As with human beings, these hi-tech scientific machines, alleged to be devoid of personality, need a complete rest from time to time. Log out, turn if off, give it a rest, and then fire it up again; it'll probably work. I know this sounds strange, but the Web and browsers are not user friendly 100% of the time!

The Web is a growing, rapidly changing thing. There's no guarantee that a Web site you found yesterday will still be there tomorrow — and likewise, no guarantee that the Web sites that I recommend in this book will necessarily still be there when you try to find them.

Surf's up

Now that you know how to ring the bells and blow the whistles, it's time to play a tune. Surf with abandon — play with the buttons and pull-down menus to find out what they do! See what you can find! Let the kid in you come out. Go ahead, you can't break the machine or screw up the program! You'll be surprised at how easy it is to use these comprehensive, Web-embracing browsers. Click on *What's New?* and *What's Cool?*, then try *Net Search*.

The beauty of most browsers is their similarity. Most have nearly identical functions, although the terminology for their buttons and options may differ. Netscape and Internet Explorer are the cool browsers this week — but next year? Who knows? I contend that if you have worked with either one of these browsers, you will be able to work with any of the newer browsers as they are developed.

Don't read this part yet!

At the beginning of this chapter, I imply that the World Wide Web is the future. I also say that gopher, ftp, and telnet will soon be things of the past. It's nearly that way now. Unless you know about gopher, ftp, and telnet, the next couple of paragraphs will be meaningless to you, so skip right over them if you like, until you've read chapter 7; then come back and read this page.

Here's why using a Web browser is better than all the other programs put together. If you want to access a file in GopherSpace, you do not need to change navigation programs — stay in your browser. At the URL prompt, type *gopher://* in lowercase letters, followed by the address you want in GopherSpace. When you hit *Return*, a familiar looking set of gopher files will appear, and you can surf away in GopherSpace using your browser.

The same is true for ftp. At the URL prompt, type *ftp://* and the address you want from ftp or Fetch. The same prompts for ftp will appear, and you take it from there. This is so much easier than having to work with three or four different navigation programs. The beauty of a Web browser is the ease with which you can go anywhere on it.

Why don't you give this a try? In your browser, Open this site:

ERIC — Educational Resources Information Center

URL: gopher://ericir.syr.edu

To "work" a gopher screen like the one above, just click on any of the file folders and you will be transported to that item. I recommend that you try "Lesson Plans" and see what ERIC has to offer. You'll be pleasantly surprised.

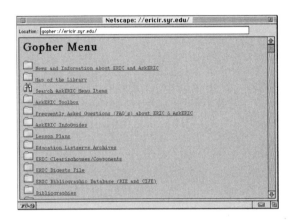

In your classroom

In this chapter, I offer you no other "lesson plan" than this: After you have surfed with your browser for a while, take your new found knowledge to your classroom and demonstrate the power of the Internet to your kids. Show them some of the things you have discovered thus far. Share your excitement and amazement with your kids. If you are brave, set yourself and your kids free. Let everyone see what everyone else comes up with! This is a tough lesson to evaluate, but you should be able to see eyes wide open in wonder and fascination, and you'll hear lots of noise! If you see and hear the above, the lesson was successful!

Notes

_____

_____

_____

_____

_____

_____

_____

Chapter 3

A Wealth of Web Sites

The Web has thousands of resources, but my favorites are the megapages. A megapage is a Web site that contains links to lots of different sites. They are handy directories that someone has created to help you find "things" in a hurry. A great way to find tons of information and even more resources is to find some key megapages and then surf away.

With so many sites on the Internet, and each better than the one before, it would be pointless to try to say which ones are best. In this chapter, you'll find about a hundred Web sites that you just cannot afford to miss if you're seeking resources for teaching. Some of them contain ready-made lesson plans, and others supply you with the information you need to design goal-oriented lessons that meet your objectives. Most of the sites are free, so click on *Open* and start typing in URLs. While there are a few Web sites that do have a registration fee, most will have a "freebie" area for folks like you and me.

I have organized the following megapages not in order of importance, but according to some basic curricular areas, except the first one, which offers general K-12 resources.

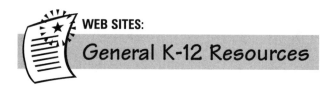

WEB SITES:
General K-12 Resources

Carrie's Crazy Quilt — Sites for Educators

> URL: http://www.mtjeff.com/~bodenst/page5.html

This all-purpose Web site offers curriculum resources in every area of study. Carrie Bodensteiner is a high school teacher, so she has a good idea of what teachers want. It is an easy-to-access Web page with something for every one. The "Sites for Educators" is just one small aspect of her Crazy Quilt, but it includes search engines, and

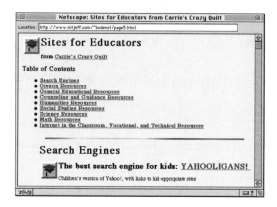

resources for Oregon, general education, counseling and guidance, humanities, social studies, science, math, Internet in the classroom, and vocational, and technical.

Kid's Web

> URL: http://www.npac.syr.edu/textbook/kidsweb/fastindex.html

This is a popular site, so don't be surprised if it is busy. The main Web site is a table of contents with listings in four general areas: Arts, Sciences, Social Studies, and Miscellaneous. Also listed are links to other digital libraries, collections of Web sites for kids, and a list of some K-12 schools on the Internet. For the truly ambitious, the link "The Classroom Internet Server Cookbook" explains how to set up a Web server in your classroom. This page is part of a Web site from Syracuse University.

A Teacher's Place

> URL: http://pluto.njcc.com/~harris

Peter Harris, a teacher and computer specialist at Robbins Elementary School in Trenton, New Jersey, has designed this page with *you* in mind. It is

a list of resources that seems to get better every time I've looked at it. Check out Links for Teachers and Parents, PJ's Page for Kids, Newsgroups for Teachers, and Schools and Teachers on the Net. It's a good location to bookmark.

Common Knowledge Pittsburgh

URL: http://info.pps.pgh.pa.us/local.html

The main page is a 12-box matrix with all sorts of information about Pittsburgh Public Schools. But I like the box labeled "Internet Resources," which has its own URL at http://info.pps.pgh.pa.us/k12/www.html. Here you can find other schools on the net and general education resources, as well as resources for culture, language, the arts, and more.

Cool School Tools

URL: http://gnn-e2a.gnn.com/gnn/wic/wics/teach.10.html

When I first saw the title of this Web site, I wondered why I had not seen the cute little rhyme before. Once you get here click on School Resources. It will greet you with the following list of goodies: General K-12 resources, Philosophy, Social Science, Customs, Folklore, Etiquette, and History of North America. I counted over 50 categories of links, most of them useful to teachers. Need I say more!

K-12 Sources — Curriculum — Lessons Plans

URL: http://execpc.com/~dboals/k-12.html#GENERAL K-12 RESOURCES

Don't miss this Web site. When I first started going to this site, there were only 185 links to sites of an educational nature. Now there are over 250, and I'm sure the list is growing. This mini-directory has everything from the Virtual Frog Dissection Kit to Music. Don't miss this Web site. If you want to find something specific on it, use the Find button in your browser to help you out. Dennis Boals developed this site, which is linked to an even larger Web site for busy History and Social Science Teachers. You will find it at http://www.execpc.com/~dboals/boals.html.

Kathy Schrock's Guide for Educators

URL: http://www.capecod.net/Wixon/wixon.htm

Kathy's site keeps getting better and better. Here you can find resources for every curriculum area, easy to find search engines and directories, lessons about using the Internet, and more. Truly an amazing Web site and one you need to keep going back to time and again.

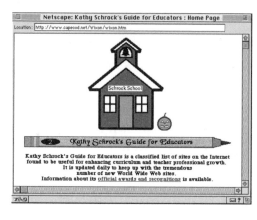

Mighty Media Resource Guide

URL: http://www.mightymedia.com/~imagemap/home?67,190

Here's what they say about their Web site: "This resource guide is aimed at providing Internet-based educators with a set of crucial pointers to valuable directories and indices about online educational resources. . . . " Then there is an alphanumeric list beginning with "4Kids" and ending with the "Youth Explorer Program." In between there are more than 50 other links to teacher resources.

Sholom's Resources for Students and Teachers

URL: http://www.interlog.com/~sholeise/ResourceTables.html

Another matrix Web site, so you need a browser that supports tables to get the best picture of this useful little resource for teachers. Sholom has divided the site into six areas: Education, Humanities, The Sciences, Computer Technology, Mother Earth, and Miscellaneous. It has an easy-to-use matrix that my students seem to like.

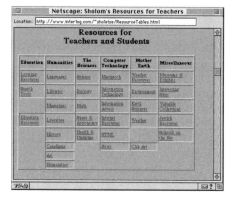

The North Dakota ICICLE Project

> URL: http://calvin.cc.ndsu.nodak.edu/wayne/icicle.html

This Web site was developed by the people in North Dakota, where it gets mighty cold. Follow the links to resources in Computer and Technology Education; Elementary Education; Fine Arts; Health, Physical Education, and Recreation; Language Arts; Mathematics; Middle School Education; Music; Science; Social Studies; Special Education; and Vocational Education.

The TradeWave Galaxy

> URL: http://www.einet.net/galaxy.html

Formerly the Einet Galaxy, this site includes links to Arts & Humanities, Business and Commerce, Community, Engineering and Technology, Government, Law, Leisure & Recreation, Medicine, Reference and Interdisciplinary Sources, Science, and Social Science. Each link leads you to education sites related to these

themes. Some Web sites refer to "The Galaxy" as a directory because it has more links than you can imagine. By the way, education is listed on this site, almost at the bottom — click on **Find** and you will be taken there straight away.

Teachers Helping Teachers

> URL: http://pacificnet.net/~mandel/index.html

The purpose of this site is threefold: 1) provide basic teaching tips to inexperienced teachers — ideas that can be immediately implemented into the classroom; 2) provide new ideas in teaching methodologies for all teachers; and 3) provide a forum for experienced teachers to share their expertise and tips with colleagues around the world. The Web site is one of the few that has a chat line for teachers.

Steve and Ruth Bennett's Family Surfboard

   URL: http://www.familysurf.com/

They created this site to help parents enjoy the fun of educational computing with their children. There is information about good sites for kids, lots of online activities, and a forum on how families can deal with computing issues in their household. It does not take a large leap of the imagination to make this page useful for teachers.

Classroom Connect

   URL: http://www.classroom.net/

Classroom Connect's site is an excellent launching pad to explore the Net. At this versatile site you can find K-12 resources on the Net, lesson plans, and lots more. This Web site is updated at least once a week — these people are serious about teaching with the Internet! I like to stop at this site

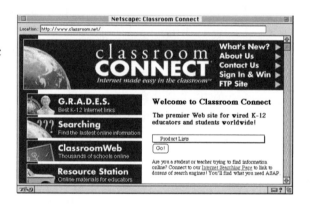

periodically just to see what's happening. You can also subscribe to the *Classroom Connect* Newsletter. Each edition is full of good information about some aspect of the Internet, as well as lesson plans, pointers to other resources, and calls for electronic keypals.

Pacific Bell Blue Web'n

   URL: http://www.kn.pacbell.com/wired/bluewebn/

A search engine with pull-down menus opens this site. Just respond to the prompts, and within seconds the results of your search will appear. Pacific Bell has collected some of the best lessons, resources, activities and projects available in science, English, math, history, art, business, and more. If you like puns, then you will appreciate the name of this Web site.

McRel Internet Connections

URL: http://www.mcrel.org/connect/

McRel stands for Mid-continent Regional Educational Laboratory, one of several regional labs across the country. It is a nonprofit organization aimed at improving the quality of education. McRel provides federally-funded services to Colorado, Kansas, Missouri, Nebraska, North Dakota, South Dakota, and Wyoming. Click on Internet Connections and find links to Special Connections, Education Resources, Subject Area Resources, Resources by State, and Internet Resources. You can also find Acceptable Use Policies.

An Educational Interface with the WWW

URL: http://www.cis.uab.edu/info/grads/mmf/EdPage/EdPage2.html

Still under construction, this site currently has links to Research Tools and Resources, Subject Index, The Teacher's Room, The Student's Room, Internet and Computer Information, Schools on the Internet, and Link Pages. I think the page holds great potential for teachers. I like the straight-forward pages with a minimum of fancy graphics, and this site meets my standards: It is easy to read, yet enjoyable to look at.

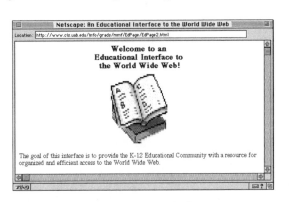

EdCentral Home Page

URL: http://www.ehhs.cmich.edu/

Provided by Central Michigan University, this site has links in three major areas: The Educational Environment, Focus on the Profession, and EdCentral. EdCentral provides teachers with different definitions of resources available on the Internet. It's definitely worth your time to look at this site.

WWW Constructivist Project Design Guide

URL: http://www.ilt.columbia.edu/k12/livetext/webcurr.html

This guide can help initiate experienced educators into designing constructivist, cooperative learning projects around the World Wide Web. You will find links to Global Studies, American Studies, Language Arts, Math, Science, Media Studies, ESL/Other Languages, and a Kid's Page.

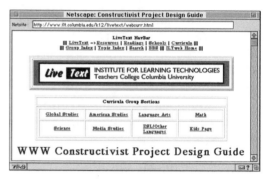

What's on the Web

URL: http://edweb.sdsu.edu/edfirst/applications/WebCUE.html

The most unusual of all the pages listed in this chapter, this is a good essay (I know, dull and boring . . . but don't judge ahead of time) about the Internet and how you can use it. There are links to various Web sites, and the information is useful.

The New Jersey Curriculum Home Page

URL: http://njnie.dl.stevens-tech.edu/curriculum/currichome.html

This site contains lesson plans and online tutorials in various subject areas. It is part of a larger New Jersey in Education Web site — which is good, even if specific to New Jersey — that is truly related to curriculum we can all use.

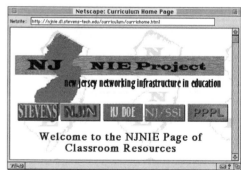

Cornell Theory Center Gateway for Teachers

URL: http://www.tc.cornell.edu/Edu/MathSciGateway/educGateway.html

Designed in blues, gray, and black, I find this site restful because it does not offer lots of moving script or loud colors. Since people found out how easy it is to make colorful web pages with sound and moving and animated *.gifs*,

it's almost impossible to find a straightforward page, but this is one of them! I wish for more like this one. It has resources for math and science as the URL indicates, but there are also resources in the humanities and arts.

Steve's Dump

URL: http://forum.swarthmore.edu/~steve/steve/education.html

This page has grown over the past year, and it has become better organized. Don't let the title turn you away from some useful general education resources for field trips, lesson plans, ERIC digests, and more. Bookmark it! You'll hear about this site again, as it is linked to Steve's Math Forum, which I'll talk about later.

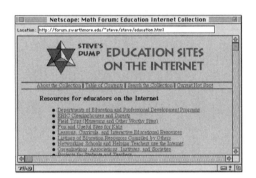

Curriculum Storehouses with a Twist

URL: http://www.songline.com/teachers/storehouses.html

Instead of a list of lists, this site contains annotations on some good storehouses of information for you, the teacher. Check out the Montessori Education Page and Houghton-Mifflin's Educational Place as just two examples of resources available to you.

 WEB SITES:

Governmental Department of Education Sites

The Departments of Education in several states have posted huge resource pages with lots of links they think will be helpful to educators. I list some of them below, but you can search for other State Departments of Education by going to:

The State Government on the Net

URL: http://www.webcom.com/~piper/state/states.html

Other Department of Education sites are:

Colorado Department of Education

    URL: http://www.cde.state.co.us/

Information about Colorado is nice, but click on Electronic Resources and Information and Interesting Sites for Students, Teachers, and Others.

California Department of Education Goldmine

    URL: http://goldmine.cde.ca.gov/

Go here for information on California curriculum frameworks, California legislation as it relates to schools and education, and links to lesson plans and other resources.

TENET Web

    URL: http://www.tenet.edu:80/

Texas does things in a big way, and this is a big site. If you are a registered TENET user, the whole site is accessible. If not, you can browse the TENET gopher (click on it), which is a pretty good consolation prize.

U.S. Department of Education

    URL: http://www.ed.gov/

Read the mission statement of the Department of Education and the National Educational Goals, access education guides, and gopher to "other educational resources."

WEB SITES:

And Now a Word from ERIC

ERIC Clearinghouse on Reading, English and Communication

URL: http://www.indiana.edu/~eric_rec/index.html

Click on any of the links to find out about Ask ERIC, ERIC digests, the Family Literacy Center, and, if you click on Distance Education Program, you will find reference to a three-unit class on the Internet called "The Online Classroom."

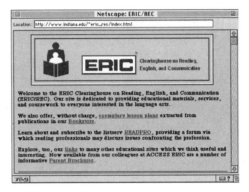

Ask ERIC

URL: http://ericir.syr.edu/

There are more than 20 ERIC clearinghouses across the country, each dealing with a separate database of knowledge. This is the "main" ERIC clearinghouse Web site. At this site you can search the database, Ask ERIC, tour a virtual library, and more. It has a large graphic at the beginning, which does take some time to download, but if you are impatient,

the same information is written below the graphic. Take your pick how you want to view the page.

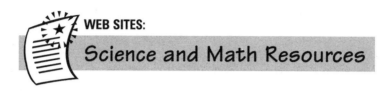

WEB SITES:
Science and Math Resources

Useful Science Web Sites

> URL: http://www.hkstar.com/~hkiedsci/de-web.htm

This Hong Kong Web site includes 26 links to other science sites. It is part of a larger site called Digital Electronics, which has a tutorial lesson for high school electronics. You can find it at URL: http://home.hkstar.com/~hkiedsci/

Virtual Library: General Resources

> URL: http://euclid.math.fsu.edu/Science/General.html

Here are more than 60 math and science links. Some of them are good, others I would skip. Scan the list and see which links fit your needs. This is part of a larger Virtual Library site at URL: http://www.w3.org/pub/DataSources/bySubject/Overview.html.

The Why Files

> URL: http://whyfiles.news.wisc.edu/

This online newspaper tries to explain the science behind the headlines. Surf here and click on previous issues, sports and science, a cool science image, and a Q/A forum.

Science Learning Network

> URL: http://www.sln.org/

Click on resources and find lessons about water, hurricanes, and the wind.

NASA (National Aeronautics and Space Administration)

URL: http://www.nasa.gov/NASA_homepage.html

NASA offers a wealth of goodies for teachers and students, and there are links to many other sites of scientific interest. There also are other excellent NASA sites on the Web, and you can get to them from here. You'll probably find these sites busy at all times of the day and night. I've been successful about one out of three times I've tried. It's worth the wait.

The Nine Planets: A Multimedia Tour of our Solar System

URL: http://seds.lpl.arizona.edu/billa/tnp/

At this comprehensive examination of our solar system, you will find links to just about everything now known about our nine planets. It also includes information about moons, orbits, the Hubble telescope and its photos of outer space, and much more. Turn your budding scientists loose, and give the world its first extraterrestrial colonists!

The Messier Science Page

URL: http://seds.lpl.arizona.edu/messier/Messier.html

From 1758 to 1782, Charles Messier, a French astronomer, compiled a list of a 100 diffuse objects that he thought were comets. As it turned out, the "comets" were nebulae, star clusters and other beautiful objects found in the night sky. Go to this site to see some excellent graphics on the wonders of the night sky.

Stars and Galaxies

URL: http://www.eia.brad.ac.uk/btl/sg.html

This site tries to explain how stars and galaxies behave, their origins and life cycle, and how they generate energy. An audio portion at the beginning will take about two minutes to download.

Welcome to the Planets

URL: http://pds.jpl.nasa.gov/planets/

A tour of our Solar System from the Jet Propulsion Lab and the California Institute of Technology, this site complements the Nine Planets Web site.

Virtual Frog Dissection Kit

URL: http://george.lbl.gov/ITG.hm.pg.docs/dissect/info.html

The University of California at Berkeley and the Lawrence Livermore Labs offer a good way to familiarize your students with the anatomy of the frog, without having to breathe formaldehyde or handle a dead frog (a major disappointment, I admit, to a true-hearted future biologist). The Dissection Kit is a superb application

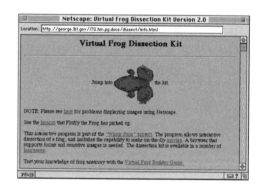

of virtual reality to classroom learning. Since this "kit" was developed, a few more have shown up.

The Cow's Eye Dissection

URL: http://www.exploratorium.edu/learning_studio/cow_eye/

Along with a step-by-step lesson on the anatomy of a cow's eye, there is a short audio introduction at the beginning that has laughing kids and statements such as "gross." But hang in there, the purpose of this anatomy lesson is to learn more about how the eye works.

The Visible Human Project

> URL: http://www.nlm.nih.gov/research/visible/visible_human.html

The goal of this project is to create a three-dimensional view of a human male and human female. While quite complex, it is interesting. The Web site requires a browser that can interpret Java (see Chapter 6).

Archeology Resources

> URL: http://www.interlog.com/~jabram/elise/archmenu.htm

Kids like digging around, so archeology can be quite fascinating. For a comprehensive listing about archeology, check out what the Royal Ontario Museum has to offer. I especially like the link titled "What is Archeology?"

But there are many other useful links at this site, too. "Pieces of the Past, Archeology Exercises" is also much fun. See URL: http://www.rom.on.ca/eeducate/zarchhis.htm

Rainforest Workshop

> URL: http://164.116.102.2/mms/rainforest_home_page.html

Here you can visit four different types of rainforests and lots of resources and lessons. This site was developed by Virginia Reid and her middle school students, and it is maintained by one of the students. A great example of what kids can do on the Internet!

Honolulu Community College Dinosaur Exhibit

URL: http://www.hcc.hawaii.edu/dinos/dinos.1.html

Dinosaurs in Hawaii? Yes. This great museum exhibit has pictures of dinosaurs and a guided audio tour.

SAMI (Science and Math Initiatives)

URL: http://www.c3.lanl.gov/~jspeck/SAMI-home.shtml

I have found that math-only sites are difficult to find, but SAMI has some. The "chatback line," "mathematics and science curricula," "other resources," and "rural resources" are all worth viewing. Click on Lesson Plans and Projects, and find a list of links to both math and science.

Virtual Library: Mathematics Gophers

URL: http://euclid.math.fsu.edu/Science/Gophers.html

This list of mathematics resources in GopherSpace is not fancy, but the resources are useful.

Geometry Center Welcome Page

URL: http://www.geom.umn.edu/

The University of Minnesota and the National Science Foundation have created this Web site devoted to K-16 education. The material ranges from easy to complex. One of the lessons has to do with building rainbows.

The Pi Page

URL: http://www.ccsf.caltech.edu/~roy/pi.html

Everything you ever wanted to know about Pi, including the first 50,000 digits of Pi. There is even a section on the uselessness of Pi.

WEB SITES:

English/Reading/Language Arts Resources

Shakespeare Headquarters

   URL: http://the-tech.mit.edu/Shakespeare.html

If you are studying the Bard, you must visit this Web site just to see a complete list of his comedies, tragedies, sonnets, and poems, along with a wonderful interactive glossary. When you are reading the text and you come across a word you do not know, click on it, and the glossary will appear telling you what the word meant during Shakespeare's time.

Global Show-n-Tell Exhibit

   URL: http://www.telenaut.com/gst/

At this Web site primary and elementary students can share with others what they have written or drawn about their favorite possessions, projects, and accomplishments. There are stories, drawings, and home pages of other little kids like yours. The beauty of the site is the ease with which you can fold it gently into your class,  and your students can add their own show-and-tell to the site.

The Children's Literature Web Guide

   URL: http://www.ucalgary.ca/~dkbrown/index.html

This excellent Web site offers all sorts of links to good children's literature. There are also links for teachers, parents, storytellers, and kids. You are bound to find something of interest to you or your kids.

Internet Public Library Story Hour

URL: http://ipl.sils.umich.edu/youth/StoryHour/

It's a link from the larger Internet Public Library Web site. Here, you can read some online stories and look at pictures related to the stories.

KidPub WWW Publishing

URL: http://www.en-garde.com/kidpub/

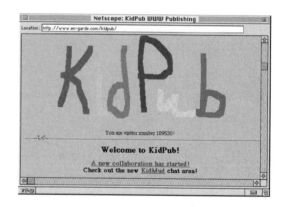

I was visitor number 150, 599 . . . so it's popular. At this site kids can publish their stories. Seems like a natural for many elementary classrooms. Check this URL out and get some ideas.

Kids' Space

URL: http://plaza.interport.net/kids_space/

Another place where kids can show off their writing, painting, and thinking to others. If you are looking to publish your kids' work, search no more.

The Writers BBS

URL: http://www.writersbbs.com/

At this poetry and prose bulletin board for writers of all ages, there are several free pages for authors.

Roget's (1911) Thesaurus

URL: http://www2.thesaurus.com/thesaurus/

You know Roget's Thesaurus. Well, now it's online — only it's the 1911 version. I find that this is an interesting site that some of your students may enjoy.

 WEB SITES:

Resources Related to Interactive Projects

With more classrooms becoming connected to the Internet, there are more and more interactive projects "out there." I can't try to describe all the projects that are on the Internet, but I will provide you with some URLs. The oldest is The Jason Project (which is now seven going on eight years old — an oldtimer in the Net world).

The Jason Project

> URL: http://seawifs.gsfc.nasa.gov/scripts/JASON.html

Where on the Globe is Roger?

> URL: http://www.gsn.org/gsn/proj/rog/index.html

Roger and his car Bubba go all over the world. Your kids can go with Roger as he travels to Austria, Russia, Australia . . . and just about everywhere. Your kids will learn about money exchange rates, languages, food, and culture, and they can ask Roger questions along the way.

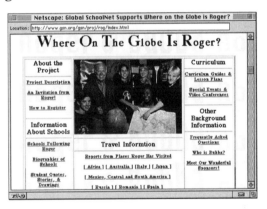

MayaQuest 96

> URL: http://www.mecc.com/mayaquest.html

MayaQuest has been Shockwaved. That means the introduction has 3D effects and music (see Chapter 6). MayaQuest 97 will start in March, but you can still visit to look at past experiences with the MayaQuest team.

Academy One

URL: http://www.nptn.org:80/
cyber.serv/AOneP
/internet.html

Check this site out for projects that
involve every area of the
curriculum. This is a must see.

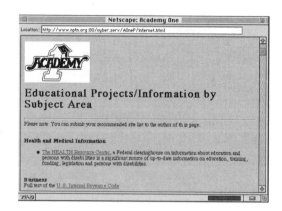

Odyssey in Egypt

URL: http://www.scriptorium.org/odyssey/

This site has information about a 10-week archeological dig in Egypt in
1996. Plans are being made for the 1997 dig. Check it out; you might want
your students to get involved.

Online Projects

URL: http://www.songline.com/teachers/online.html

In case I missed any projects, this is the master list of most of them.

WEB SITES:

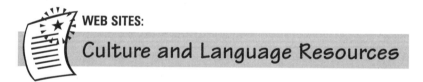 Culture and Language Resources

The Internet is about communicating with other people — whether your best
friend next door or with people around the world whom you'll never meet except
virtually on the Internet. Contrary to the often heard idea that computers
depersonalize learning, computers do more to put learners in contact with other
learners, and people with people, than any other communication medium. Help
your students achieve global interpersonal dialogue by building keypal
relationships and by plugging into Web sites that link your students to other
people and other cultures.

World Cultures

URL: http://info.pps.pgh.pa.us/k12/culture.html

If you want to reach out and touch a culture, check out this site. There are links to lots of other sites dealing with the various aspects of human cultures: General World, African-American, Asian, European, Libraries and Exhibits, and the Americas. You can tour the Kremlin or Paris, go to several UNESCO heritage sites, view the symbols of Malaysia (national flag, car, etc.), or journey into China, and more.

Human Languages Page

URL: http://www.willamette.edu/~tjones/Language-Page.html

Tyler Jones is the guru of languages. He improves this site all the time. At this single URL you can find out something about almost every language spoken on earth. Check out the easy ones first, such as Spanish or French, and then try any other language you can think of — Croatian or Basque or Afrikaans — including languages that are no longer spoken, such as Middle English.

 **WEB SITES:**

Appalachian State College Sites

The following sites are at Appalachian State College Department of Languages. Each includes information about course offerings, and the culture the language represents.

General Language Page

URL: http://www.acs.appstate.edu/dept/fll/index.html

The French Page at URL: http://www.acs.appstate.edu/dept/fll/french.html

The Spanish Page at URL: http://www.acs.appstate.edu/dept/fll/spanish.html

The Chinese Page at URL: http://www.acs.appstate.edu/dept/fll/chinese.html

The Russian Page at URL: http://www.acs.appstate.edu/dept/fll/russian.html

The Latin Page at URL: http://www.acs.appstate.edu/dept/fll/latin.html

The Japanese Page at URL: http://www.acs.appstate.edu/dept/fll/japanese.html

The ESL Page at URL: http://www.acs.appstate.edu/dept/fll/esl.html

WEB SITES:
History and Social Science Resources

Social Studies Lesson Plans for Teacher

URL: http://www.csun.edu/%7Ehcedu013/index.html

Dr. Marty Levine has developed this site with social studies teachers in mind. It has links to lesson plans, resources, and current events.

Teaching Resources for Historians

URL: http://www.csun.edu/%7Ehcedu013/index.html

From here you can link to Web sites about the American Revolution, the Jewish Holocaust in Europe, Archeology, and several other subjects of historical interest. This link falls under the Web site for the Association of History and Computing at http://grid.let.rug.nl/ahc/welcome.html

The History Home Page

URL: http://www.panix.com/~steel/

Bob Steel, a social studies teacher at Rye High School in Rye, New York, has developed this site for history teachers. Because surf time is hard to find, he has created this directory to Internet-related history and social studies sites.

The Social Studies Page

URL: http://howww.ncook.k12.il.us/docs/socstd.html

At this big site with links to economics, geography, government, history and people, you can find the CIA Fact Book, as well as a tour of the Grand Canyon.

Social Studies School Service

URL: http://www.socialstudies.com

This major social studies site is a quick way to find all the other social studies and history sites, plus other print and CD-ROM resources.

History Buff's Home Page

URL: http://www.serve.com/ephemera/historybuff.html

Devoted to newspaper stories that have historical interest, this site starts with a cute graphic of a library. By clicking on the stacks, you go to various places. I was interested in the story about Tad Lincoln, but there are also other stories about the Civil War, the circus, the Old West, and believe it not, wallpaper.

History Social Science K-12 WebPage

URL: http://www.execpc.com/~dboals/boals.html

This home page is devoted to History and Social Science. It would be a life long adventure just going through all the Web sites at this one URL.

1492 Exhibit

URL: http://sunsite.unc.edu/expo/ 1492.exhibit/Intro.html

This Library of Congress exhibit that follows the 1492 voyage of Christopher Columbus includes maps and graphics.

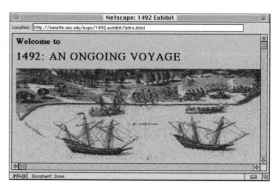

American Revolution to Reconstruction

URL: http://grid.let.rug.nl/~welling/usa/revolution.html

Part of a series on American History, this is an interesting site with lots of color. I'm biased, however, because I was a history major.

American Civil War Home Page

URL: http://funnelweb.utcc.utk.edu/~hoemann/cwarhp.html

The American Civil War is studied in the fifth, eighth and 10th or 11th grades in most districts. Recently dry and dusty old history lessons have come to life thanks to a PBS documentary. With timelines, maps, documents, diaries written by young and old alike, and pictures, this site is

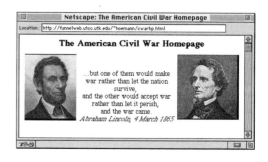

a big hit with middle school teachers. But if you teach any aspect of American History, you will want to add this site to your list of bookmarks.

Welcome to the Civil War Center

URL: http://www.cwc.lsu.edu/

To complement the American Civil War Page, you must visit the Civil War Center. These folks have provided more than 1,000 links to information about one of the bloodiest wars in our history. There are movie clips, audio files, and other goodies here as well.

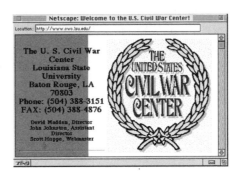

Suffrage History

URL: http://www.pbs.org:80/onewoman/suffrage.html

Mostly text, this PBS site tells the history of women's suffrage.

National Flags

URL: http://155.187.10.12/flags/nation-flags.html

If your kids are doing reports on nations around the world, then they need this site. You can get images of flags from Argentina to Zambia, and more flags are being added on a regular basis.

CapWeb — A Guide to the U.S. Congress

URL: http://policy.net/capweb/congress.html

To get access to the Senate and House of Representatives, visit this URL. There are also other links to the federal government from this site. Another similar site is THOMAS, named for Thomas Jefferson. You will find it at URL: http://loc.thomas.gov/

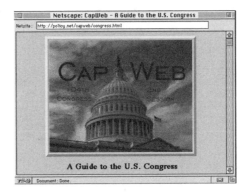

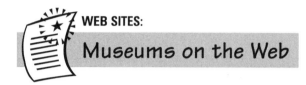

Exploratorium Home Page

 URL: http://isaac.exploratorium.edu/

Visit the San Francisco Exploratorium at the Palace of Fine Arts. You can click on the World of Science and the Learning Studio to go to new worlds of information.

Ocean Planet Home Page

 URL: http://seawifs.gsfc.nasa.gov/ocean-planet.html

This Smithsonian exhibit looks at the power of the ocean. To quote them, "it plumbs the depths of the watery world". . . but I wouldn't want to go that far. The many facets of this site will take a bit of time to explore.

Resources at the Smithsonian

 URL: http://www.si.edu/resource/start.htm

If you liked the Ocean Planet, then you might like to search the Smithsonian for other exhibits and resources. Click on Open and type in the URL above, and the nation's attic will be at your fingertips.

Franklin Institute of Science Museum

 URL: http://sln.fi.edu/tfi/welcome.html

The first online museum I entered is still one of my favorites. Here you can find lessons, science demonstrations, online exhibits, and just plain fun.

WebMuseum

   URL: http://www.zmall.com/wm/

Perhaps the most famous museum of
the Internet, you will see exhibits
change periodically (keep going back
to catch up on the great Masters).
You can also take a quick tour of
Paris. There are also numerous
mirror sites to the WebMuseum,
because it is so popular. The above
URL is for one of the many mirror sites of the WebMuseum.

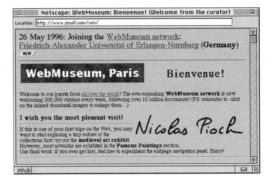

WEB SITES:

School Sites

There are lots of megapages developed by elementary, middle school, and high
school students and/or teachers. I find these sites interesting, because they give me
ideas for lessons, projects, and developing home pages.

K-12 World Wide Web Sites

   URL: http://www.sendit.nodak.edu/k12/

Many schools that are online are
listed at this Web site. After you have
made up your home page, you can
add it to this site, too. It's fun to see
your school listed on another Web
site. In addition, you can browse the
home pages out there for many good
ideas about lessons and activities you
can do with the Internet.

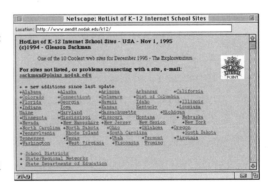

Vose School Educational Resources

URL: http://www.teleport.com/~vincer/starter.html

This example of a home page designed and maintained by a school is a standard to aspire to! Vose School presents you with more resources than you will have time to use. Some of them are duplicates found on other lists, and some are unique to Vose. I especially like the "Kidopedia" — an encyclopedia designed by kids for kids to use.

Beyond screens full of information, teachers and students share with one another what they are doing on the Internet. Lesson plans, work done by the kids, ideas that you can adapt for your classroom — if it works for Vose, it'll work for you. Vince Ruggiano, Vose's Webmaster, updates the site regularly and keeps the wealth of information timely for Vose teachers and for you. Recently the site started using a frame format, so you will need a browser that supports frames to see the true value of this Web site.

Project City Elementary School Home Page

URL: http://www.shastalink.k12.ca.us/projectcity/PCHOMEPAGE.html

There are many places of interest on this home page. Check out the World Wide Creative Writing Project and the Blue Rivers of Salmon Project. Your students will have fun participating in one or both of them. There are links to projects, resources, and fun things for kids to do. Just scroll down the Project City Elementary School Home Page and you will find something of interest.

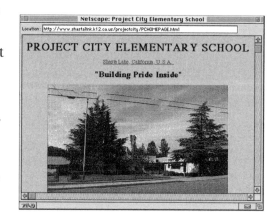

How to Teach Using the Internet

I bet you can hardly wait to get started. Before you do, there are three things to think about: 1) acceptable use policies (AUP), 2) room arrangements, and 3) lesson planning. These three things are not nearly as much fun as looking at Web sites and deciding what you are going to do with them.

You know that the Internet is a handy tool to find references and resources from all over the world. You were just given a wealth of sites from which to choose, and I hope you have a good idea how to use both your computer and the browser program that you have installed.

The first time I did a workshop I thought I had it all figured out, until I was led into a beautiful Macintosh lab with 30 computers, all a little different from each other. I did not know how to turn on 10 of the computers. Lucky for me, I knew my browser, Netscape, and the lesson went much better than the initial panic of not being able to help folks turn their computers on!

Learn how to use your computer and your browser program before you start letting your kids get online. There's a good reason for this: Your kids may know more about the Internet than you will, (which is great, since they are a resource you can use) but you may have to bail them out. If you don't know the computers or the programs, you are stuck.

Creating an Acceptable Use Policy

While you are learning all about your computer and the browser program you are using, you should also be studying AUPs. These are the policies that must be in place to assure parents, teachers, and students that you are using the Internet for educational and curricular purposes. There are many sample AUPs on the Web. I suggest you look at a number written by other teachers before writing one and having it approved by your school.

See some of these sites for acceptable use policies:

URL: http://152.30.11.86/deer/Houghton/edel666/F95/Fuchs3/
HOMEPAGE.HTML#examples

URL: gopher://riceinfo.rice.edu:1170/11/More/Acceptable

URL: http://www.songline.com/teachers/usepolicies.html

Also check out:

Parent's Guide
URL: http://www.cais.net/cannon/memos/parents.htm

The Bill of Rights for Electronic Learners
URL: http://spacelink.msfc.nasa.gov/Instructional.Materials/
Video.and.Activity.Guides/Connecting.to.the.Future.Video.Guide/
Part.8.Appendices/Section.4

Street Smart on the Web
URL: http://www.yahooligans.com/docs/safety

After you have developed the AUP, inform your students, their parents and your school administers about your policies. Have your students and their parents sign the AUP and then stick to it. I know this is difficult to do, especially if one of your super-kids breaks the policy, but it has to be done.

There is much concern about kids getting into X-rated or questionable Web sites, and you need to have an AUP in place to assure parents that you are not aiding and abetting any questionable situations. I am not for censorship on the Internet just as I am not for censorship of books, because, like a library, the Internet has a wealth of information meant for all people. I am for teaching kids the appropriate "surfing" behavior they have to use in my classroom.

When your students and their parents have signed the AUP, you need to give your students time to practice using the computer and the Internet. They need it as much as you did. In the best of all worlds, you have one computer for every two

kids, but that is a dream that may not happen any time in the near future. You will probably have between one and four computers in your room, and if you are lucky all of them will be connected to the Internet. I like to have two students work together. The Internet is an interactive medium, so let two kids interact with it. This will lead to some noisy activities, so be prepared.

Getting Organized

You do not have to change the desks in the room to accommodate the computers, but you do need to have all the computer screens facing toward you. While it might look neater to have all the computers in a "private" area, or facing toward the back of the room, it is not a place where you can monitor what is happening on a regular basis. Also, computers with screens facing the back of the room tend to have more games played on them, and that is not the whole purpose of having a computer on the Internet in your classroom.

If you want to change the room arrangement, I've found that computers placed along the sides of the room facing toward the center of the room affords me a good view of all the screens with just a quick glance. It does have the drawback that everyone else can see the screen too, which can be distracting if you are trying to teach one group of kids while another group is visiting a great Web site.

The next thing I do is change the font size on my browser. In Netscape you do this by pulling down the Options menu, clicking on General Preferences. Here you will see a series of file folders. Click on Font and change the size from 12 to 24. If you are using Internet Explorer, there are two buttons on the screen that adjust font size, click on the one that makes fonts larger.

While you are modifying font size, you might want to think about modifying the volume too. Many the newer Web sites have great audio, but how much audio can you stand? Figure out what is best for you and your class, and follow that. For me, I have the volume on as low as it will go as I don't deal with distractions very well. Volume by the way is a function of your computer and not a function of your browser.

After you have an AUP and the physical arrangement of computers and desks figured out, you need to do some analysis as to the type of lessons you want to teach. Not every lesson is "Internet compatible." According to the folks at *Classroom Connect* (http://www.classroom.net/), the best lessons are research oriented, because advanced or higher-order thinking skills occur, and allow students to compare and contrast strategies. I contend that every one of your Internet lessons has to have a rationale, objectives, and a way to evaluate the outcome. You have to know every aspect of the lesson and be able to justify why it is important to your students' learning.

While surfing the Internet is much fun, if it is not goal oriented, it is merely practice using the tool. Because you are using this tool as a teaching device, you want your kids to use their time wisely and well, and you want to be able to evaluate the product of their learning in a logical and useful way.

Given the last few paragraphs, now's the time to *do it*! The Internet is the most comprehensive collection of resources you will ever have access to and it definitely belongs in your classroom *now*.

Chapter 4

Searching on the Web

You have worked with your browser on the Internet, had a chance to look at some of the Web sites listed, and you're thinking "This is fun!" And it is! But you might be wondering how you find something when there is not a convenient URL to follow? Good question. That, by the way, is the topic of this chapter. You are going to learn how to search the Web using directories and search engines.

Remember that old saying "Give a person a fish, feed him for a day; teach a person to fish, feed him for a lifetime?" Chapter 3 was the fish, and while those "fish" will keep you busy for quite a few days, they did not teach you how to fish. So let's learn how to "fish the Web."

Two ways to find information

The Web is big and growing larger every day. Fortunately, there are a couple of ways to help you find the information you want. There are directories and search engines, and you need to know how to use both. Both are easy to use and both provide you with the same type of information (although frequently not exactly the same information).

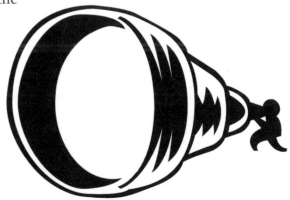

When you are learning how to define words, you use a dictionary. When you want to know something about a particular event, you use an encyclopedia. When you want to find several words that mean the same thing, you use a thesaurus. When you want to find the geographical location of a country, you use an atlas. Each source provides information in its own particular way. To use them, you learned about alphabetical order, guide words, latitude, and longitude, and you spent hours finding things in dictionaries, encyclopedias, thesauri, and atlases. The same is almost true for directories and search engines.

You don't need guide words to make the Internet directories and search engines work for you. What you do need is a sense of logic.

Directories and search engines both live on the Web as full-fledged Web sites. They have URLs like every Web site listed in this book. You can get to any directory and search engine the same way you get to any other Web site. Click on *Open* or the *Open File* icon in your browser, type in the URL, and hit *return*. It's easy. What's harder is understanding why two devices, search engines and directories, provide the same information.

Directories and Search Engines

Let's look at one directory and one search engine so you can see for yourself. The directory I have chosen is:

> *Yahoo*
>
> URL: http://www.yahoo.com/

The search engine I have chosen is:

> *Alta Vista*
>
> URL: http://altavista.digital.com/

Yahoo is the largest, oldest, and most used directory on the Internet. The Alta Vista search engine returns a lot of information in an easy-to-read format. Both sites are commercial ventures, and advertising is what pays for their development.

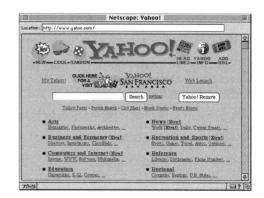

The Yahoo Web site shown on the previous page has some cute graphics that link to *What's New?*, *What's Cool?*, and other fun information. Then comes the advertisement. After that is a box with a *Search* button next to it, and following that are two columns of words called categories.

In each category there are subcategories. If, for example, you want to find the phone number of a friend in Minneapolis, click on *phone numbers* under the category of *Reference*. From there you will see a list of more subcategories, narrowing down the field until you finally find the Minneapolis phone book. Or, if you are seeking information about Frank Lloyd Wright, click on *Architecture* under the *Art* category and soon another screen appears that lists topics about architecture. You then select a subcategory that narrows the search down even farther. You keep narrowing your search until you find all the Web sites that Yahoo has screened that deal with Frank Lloyd Wright.

A search engine goes about this process in another way. The Alta Vista Web site is here. It has the required advertisement, a pretty picture (I like mountains), and a box for *Advanced Search*, *Simple Search*, *Surprise*, and *Help* (look at those another time . . . they are kind of fun). Read down the screen until you come to *Search* and a pull-down menu with "the Web" displayed, and a

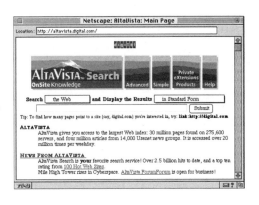

request about how you want the results displayed. Keep the choice "standard," as it's easiest. You will see a blank box. In that box you will type a key word or phrase. After typing in your key word or phrase, you press *return* or click on the *Submit* button. Soon Alta Vista will display a list of Web sites related to your key word search. Alta Vista, and all the other search engines, use key words or phrases to narrow your search pattern. Directories are based on a categorical hierarchy from general to specific. So in the Alta Vista search engine, if you were looking for your friend in Minneapolis, you would type in **Minneapolis Telephone Book**, and see what happens. If you were looking for information about Frank Lloyd Wright, you'd type in **Frank Lloyd Wright**, and see what results.

Because Alta Vista and other search engines hope to be helpful, you'll see a rating of the "hit." The rating shows how well the search engine "thinks" the hit matches your request. (Now, how a search engine can know what I want is very debatable, and how a computer can think anyway . . . but let that be for now.) In Alta Vista, the best rating is 1,000 and the poorest rating is 0, and is based on how many words in your search match the words in the headers and titles of the Web sites it returns. To use a directory or a search engine well, you need to practice logic. This practice in logic makes their use helpful for your kids.

Directory vs. Search Engine

Let's have some fun, and do an actual directory vs. search engine search. I'll lead you through it step by step, then we'll learn a little bit more about how these critters are developed, and how to do Boolean searches. Finally, we'll try a scavenger hunt that you can do first, then you can have your class do it.

Below are the categories and subcategories that Yahoo is using right now.

• Arts
Humanities, Photography, Architecture, . . .

• Business and Economy [Xtra!]
Directory, Investments, Classifieds, . . .

• Computers and Internet [Xtra!]
Internet, WWW, Software, Multimedia, . . .

• Education
Universities, K-12, Courses, . . .

• Entertainment [Xtra!]
TV, Movies, Music, Magazines, . . .

• Government
Politics [Xtra!], Agencies, Law, Military, . . .

• Health
Medicine, Drugs, Diseases, Fitness, . . .

• News [Xtra!]
World [Xtra!], Daily, Current Events, . . .

• Recreation and Sports [Xtra!]
Sports, Games, Travel, Autos, Fishing, . . .

• Reference
Libraries, Dictionaries, Phone Numbers, . . .

• Regional
Countries, Regions, U.S. States, . . .

• Science
CS, Biology, Astronomy, Engineering, . . .

• Social Science
Anthropology, Sociology, Economics, . . .

• Society and Culture
People, Environment, Religion, . . .

Let's search for information on Frank Lloyd Wright. He was an architect, so click on *Architecture* under *Arts*. From there you will find the following a list of subcategories that looks something like this:

Directories (10)
Indices (16)

- Architects (110)
- Architectural History (5)
- Books@
- Buildings and Projects (134)
- Civil Engineering@
- Companies@
- Countries and Cultures (16)
- Courses (7)
- Events (21)
- Exhibits (12)

- Forums (4)
- Institutes (102)
- Landscape Architecture (31)
- Magazines@
- Museums (8)
- Organizations (58)
- Publishers@
- Resources (8)
- Software (5)
- Urban Planning@

This list of subcategories has something to do with architecture. You might notice there are (numbers) after some of the listings, which means there are that many links when you click on that subcategory. If there is @ after some links, it means that if you click on this category, you will be given a list of other related subcategories and a list of links. When you come across an @, you know you are almost at the end of your search.

Clicking on *Architects (110)* will offer an even narrower list of sub-sub-categories:

- Companies@
- Masters (49)
- Personal Exhibits (57)
- Resumes@
- Studios (1)

You will click on *Masters (49)* because Frank Lloyd Wright was definitely a master architect. Now you have narrowed your search, because on the next screen, the last choice will be Frank Lloyd Wright. If you click on that, you will get twenty-three links. See what I mean by logic? You need to have some background information about a topic, and you need to have a general idea of where you want to go.

Now let's do the same search with the Alta Vista Search Engine (URL: http://altavista.digital.com). At the main screen, you type **Frank Lloyd Wright** in the box and click on *Submit*. Alta Vista quickly comes back with the following message:

> "Word count: Lloyd:125816; Wright:277851; Frank:499217
> Documents 1-10 of about 70000 matching some of the query terms, best matches first."

That means, Alta Vista "looked" through its database and found 125,816 matches for Lloyd; 277,851 for Wright; and 499,297 matches for Frank and 70,000 matches for all three words together on the same page; and it returned to you the 10 best matches. Each match tells you the URL, the title of the URL, and a few words about the material or information in that URL. Your job now is to select the best URLs for Frank Lloyd Wright. You have lots of choices.

In either case, with a directory or a search engine, you have to use some logic — or that uncommon quality "common sense." Also, if you look at the two sets of lists, you might notice overlap. That's good. It says you are on the right track.

What to use

Now you've tried both a directory and a search engine, and you might be asking, which is best? Let me offer you a few advantages and disadvantages for both and you can make the decision.

Pros and Cons for Directories

Directories are good browsing devices. I use them as a tool to guide me to material I might not find any other way. I like it that they are orderly, moving from general to specific information. Also, a directory is made by real people who have reviewed the sites and used some sort of selection process. For this reason, I like to use directories when I am working at schools.

There are, however, disadvantages to them. If you don't know the starting category, you might never find your information. That's why directories have a box where you can type in a key word and do a search "manually." If you don't know a specific category, use a search engine. Also, search engines provide all URLs, even those yet reviewed by people who develop the directories. New URLs are constantly being added to the Internet and it is next to impossible for reviewers to screen, categorize, and cross-reference every URL on a daily basis.

Pros and Cons for Search Engines

When you know the key word or phrase, or the specific name, a search engine is an efficient way to find information. In the Frank Lloyd Wright search, we were led directly to a list that in the end could contain 70,000 hits. That's impressive.

However, there is a drawback. You need to know a key word or phrase, and you have to be willing to look through a bunch of hits that might not be relevant to your needs.

In general, use directories for categorical searches, and search engines for key word searches. Depending on your needs, both can provide you with lots of information.

Other Web Sites for Searching the Internet

Since you are at Alta Vista, type in "search engine" in the query box. Now see how many search engines and directories are on the Web, and more are showing up daily!

I've listed a few directories and search engines below. Go to them and bookmark the ones you think you will use the most. My favorite directories are Yahoo, Magellan, A2Z, and Yahooligans. The last one is a directory made for kids, and it's really a great idea. My favorite search engines are Inktomi, WebCrawler, Lycos, InfoSeek, and Alta Vista, but these are just a few of them.

If you look at the list, note there are more search engines than directories. That's because search engines are easier to create than directories. With a directory, you need personnel to screen Web sites, put them into categories, and cross-reference the links. That's not the case with search engines.

What I look for in search engines is speed. I'm not the most patient person in the world, so I like the speedier engines better than the sluggish ones. However, some of the speediest ones also produce the most amount of garbage. Search engines look for matches to a key word. When we typed **Frank Lloyd Wright**, we got 70,000 hits. Are there really 70,000 Web sites out there that mention Frank Lloyd Wright? Or do some have Web sites Lloyd Wright or Frank Lloyd or Frank Wright or Wright Frank? You get the idea.

There is something called the "noise to hit ratio" and some search engines are famous for their "noise." Alta Vista can be a "noisy" search engine, because it will return many hits not relevant to your search. For that reason, I like to use a couple of search engines and compare and contrast their list of hits. Inktomi and WebCrawler are my two favorites, because they return fast, "not-noisy" search results.

Directories	*URLs*
A2Z	http://a2z.lycos.com/
The Magellan Internet Directory	http://www.mckinley.com:80/ mckinley-cgi/browse.pl?MAIN
Yahoo	http://www.yahoo.com/
Yahooligans	http://www.yahooligans.com/
Search Engines	URLs
Alta Vista	http://altavista.digital.com/
InfoSeek	http://home.netscape.com/escapes/ search/search1.html

Directories	URLs
Inktomi	http://inktomi.berkeley.edu/query.html
Internet Resources Meta Index	http://www.ncsa.uiuc.edu/SDG/Software/ Mosaic/MetaIndex.html
Lycos	http://www.lycos.com/
Magellan	http://www.mckinley.com/
MetaCrawler	http://metacrawler.cs.washington.edu:8080/ index.html
Open Text	http://www.opentext.com:8080
Search and Retrieval Engines and Indices	http://www.gsn.org/web/html/SOREGION/ SEARCH.htm
Search Com	http://www.search.com
Search the Entire Web	http://www.scsu-cs.ctstateu.edu/lib/worms.htm
Starting Point	http://www.stpt.com/
W3 Search Engines	http://cuiwww.unige.ch/meta-index.html
WebCrawler	http://webcrawler.com

Use each of the search engines and directories listed here, and bookmark the ones you like the best. If you want more to choose from, search for search engines using any of the search engines here, and you will be rewarded with even more!

Boolean Searches

There's one more thing to know: how to do a Boolean search. Some, not all, of the search engines listed want you to do Boolean key word searches. The first time I heard about that kind of search, I was taking my MA stats class, and I dreaded the whole thing. Well, seeing it on a search engine started the old fear right up again. Don't let it happen to you! I finally have Boolean searches down cold! And they are not even hard. Just put it down as one more thing you have to know to do a good search . . . and it's one more thing you can teach your kids. They'll thank you for it later (I bet)!

Boolean searches rely on three words called operators: and, or, not. That's all. If you open WebCrawler at http://webcrawler.com/Help/Advanced.html you will see a clean explanation of a Boolean search. I'll paraphrase it for you here. Say you want to find Web sites about elementary reading. If the search engine you're using requires Boolean operators, then you'll have the three choices listed below:

Operator	Example	What I will get back	Result
AND	elementary AND reading	Web sites that include both of the words — e.g., Web sites with both elementary AND reading.	AND will limit your search
OR	elementary OR reading	Web sites that include either of the words or both — e.g., sites with elementary OR those with reading OR those with both elementary and reading.	OR will limit your search
NOT	elementary NOT reading	Web sites that include the first word but not the second — e.g., sites with education but NOT reading.	NOT will limit your search

Boolean searches should be easy, but there is always a fly in the ointment. Some search engines, like WebCrawler, use "or" as the default operator. Other search engines use "and" as the default operator. Some don't use either. Then there is just one more little problem. Not all of them use the same operators. Some use colons (:) and commas (,) where others use (+), (-) and (\). When you are not sure what operators a particular search engine uses, read the opening paragraph on the home page of the search engine and look for something that suggests how you can improve your search results.

Most search engines have a built-in *Help!* function or a *FAQ* section that will give you information about how to develop a "good search." If there is a *Help* button, click on it. If the search engine uses a Boolean search pattern, follow the directions and use the correct operators for that search engine. When you know the right words to use for each search engine, you will be rewarded with better results.

Scavenger hunt, anyone?

Now you know that directories are categorical and search engines rely on key words. You know a little bit about Boolean searches, and you have URLs for several directories and search engines. At random, pick a URL from the list of directories and search engines above, and see if you can find the following items. Then try this same exercise with your students.

The rationale for this type of lesson is simple. If you are going to be using the Internet, you need to know how to gain access to the information. Just like guide words are necessary for using a dictionary, directories and search engines are necessary to find information on the Internet.

The procedure is easy. Introduce your kids to a directory and a search engine. Tell them about Boolean operators. Walk them through a couple of examples. Then give them a list of things they have to find. Evaluation is almost self-explanatory. If your kids find Web sites that match the hunt items, they are successful.

Now let's search for the following (answers follow):

1. What is the atomic number of uranium?

2. Where is Hollyhock House located?

3. True or False: *Robinson Carusoe* and *Alice in Wonderland* were written in the same year.

4. If you want to say "hello" to Chamorro folks on Guam, what word or phrase would you use?

5. When was Rutherford B. Hayes President of the United States?

Answers

1. 92 — I used WebCrawler and typed in Periodic Table of Elements. See http://www.cs.ubc.ca/elements/periodic-table

2. 4808 Hollywood Blvd., Los Angeles, CA — I used Yahoo, because I knew that Frank Lloyd Wright designed the house. See http://www.westworld.com/~fohh/map.html

3. False: *Robinson Carusoe* was written in 1721. See http://www.brunel.co.uk/davidw/_SIXTEEN.html#3 *Alice in Wonderland* was written in 1865. See http://www.germany.eu.net/books/carroll/alice.html

4. "Hafa Adai." I used Yahoo to search for Guam, then followed the listings. See http://www.gov.gu/index.html

5. 1877-1881 — I cheated. I knew that the White House home page had a listing of presidents, so I went there first — http://www.whitehouse.gov/WH/glimpse/presidents/html/rh19-plain.html. You can also get there with Yahoo, Government, then Presidents, which will eventually lead you to http://www.grolier.com/presidents/cards/front/19chaye.html

You can make a scavenger hunt easy or hard. You can search for answers that jump out at you or for embedded answers that your kids will have to read a bit before they know they are on the right track. You can develop hunts for people, places, and things on the Web as easily as you can develop hunts for ideas, facts, and opinions. And look at the skills your kids are using and learning. They are learning how to skim and scan a Web site for information, and that reinforces their reading skills. They are learning how to sort or categorize information, use higher order thinking skills, reinforce writing and typing skills, and the list goes on. As you can see, this really is a teaching tool.

I hope you had fun learning how to search the Internet, and hope you develop a couple of scavenger hunts for your kids to do. If you have a super successful one, email it to me at URL: mailto: ecotton@oavax.csuchico.edu. I'm looking forward to hearing from you soon!

Chapter 5

Developing and Designing a Web Page

You and your students can learn to write HTML (HyperText Mark-up Language) so that you can publish your own individual home pages, or even develop a Web site for your class, and your school. Yes, it's a computer language with special codes, but don't let that scare you away. It can be easy and — some would say — fun!

All you need to get started is a list of the HTML codes and any word processor or text editor. HTML uses embedded codes, tags placed inside text to mark graphical elements, hyperlinks, and typographic particulars. HTML is growing and changing. Teaching with the ever-expanding Web means that you have to run just to keep up! Thankfully, you only need to know about 12 HTML codes to write good Web pages, and those codes never change.

Getting Started with Tags

HTML is primarily a bookend code. If you want your books to stand up on the shelf, you need a bookend at the left and right ends of the row of books. It is the same with HTML: You need a tag at the beginning and end of any string of code. Angled brackets < > at the beginning say, "Code starts here." Angled brackets with forward slash </> says, "Code ends here." For example, the tag <b> causes text to be presented in bold letters. "B" for "bold" inside the angled brackets indicate an HTML coded command: "This is a code command: Turn on b for Bold!" When you get to the end of the word or phrase that you want bold, you key in </b> which tells the machine: "This is a code command: Turn off b for Bold!" As in <b> this text is bold! </b>.

HTML consists of many such tags: tags for headlines, tags for underlining, tags for italics, tags for titles, and tags for paragraph breaks, but don't be overwhelmed by all the tags! Most of the tags are alliterative, such as "b for bold" or "i for italics." After you've coded your first home page, your fingertips will have memorized most of the tags. Many browsers support tags that allow you to set up tables, customize backgrounds, and a few other nifty things. The problem with HTML is that it is too simple of a machine language, not too complex. If you're accustomed to setting type and desktop-publishing programs, you will find HTML and its limited range of typographic possibilities clunky.

One of the best ways to start setting up a collection of Web pages at your school is to consult the many online pages to learn how to create your own set of Web pages. You can also get an HTML guidebook in a bookstore or at the library. Listed below are a few beginning HTML sites you might want to visit.

HTML Guide by Dr. Clue (When you get to this page, click on HTML 101)	http://www.cnw.com/~drclue/Formula_One.cgi/ HTML/HTML.html
A List of HTML Tags	http://www.cosy.sbg.ac.at/~lendl/tags.html
123...Easy	http://spring-board.com/123easy/map.html
HTML Tutorial — An Overview	http://www-pcd.stanford.edu/mogens/intro/tutorial.html
The BareBones Guide to HTML	http://werbach.com/barebones/
Do It Yourself HTML (Down and Dirty Handbook)	http://metro.turnpike.net/D/DanMM/howhtm1.htm
The Web Designer (a directory of links to every aspect of HTML and Web design)	http://web.canlink.com/webdesign/
Creating Net Sites	http://home.netscape.com/assist/net_sites/index.html

Decoding Tags

One feature you'll be using is the HTML hyperlink. When you are developing your own Web site, you will want to list URLs of all sorts of Web sites for your visitors to link to from your Web page. Here's an example of HTML that puts a link in place for users to click on:

```
<A HREF="http://home.netscape.com/index.html">Home</A>
```

Now let's interpret this. The first thing you spot is the angled bracket < at the beginning that announces the start of an HTML coded command embedded in the text. Look at the end of the string and you see the other half of the pair of angled brackets with the forward slash </A>, indicating the end of the command. "A" is for "anchor," HREF stands for hypertext link or hyperlink for short, and = means "equal." It's an anchor because you're going to fix something here — like anchoring a boat, and the = sign tells you what is being anchored. The part of the tag between quotation marks "http: . . .html" is the URL of the Web page to which your readers will go if you click on that link. The text following the URL contains the highlighted text *Home* that the user sees on screen.

The code to insert images in your pages is similar to the code that commands a link to be inserted. Online images are links to image files, so instead of inserting a document that has ".html" at the end of the URL, it will have the abbreviation for the type of graphics file it is. Some of these abbreviations are ".gif," ".jpeg," or ".mpeg." Most computers will have image reading programs that support the types of image files mentioned above. So, if you are going to put in an image, you will write the following tag:

```
<img src="egc.gif">Picture of Eileen
```

Can you decode that tag?

<	The opening anchor
img src	An image source
egc.gif	File name of the graphics file
>	End of the opening anchor
Picture of Eileen	Text that will appear beside this image

If you got all of that, you are on your way to becoming an HTML programmer!

To see the HTML source code that controls anyone's Web page, just choose *View* then *Document Source* from the pull-down menus. In the PC environment you will immediately see both the tags and text that were used to make that Web page look as it does. In the Mac environment, your browser may launch an external program to show you the codes. If you have already coded a home page, the tags and text you see will have meaning to you; if you have only looked at browser screens and never delved any deeper into the medium, you may feel reading tags is like reading a foreign language. Don't let the techie jargon scare you into thinking that you cannot design and develop your own home page!

If you have surfed the Web only a little bit — especially in regions where educators roam — you probably have seen home pages written by five-year-olds, and you will certainly have seen home pages put up on the Web by elementary school kids. If kids can do it, you can do it! You do not need to be a computer programmer to develop a home page. You need only to know what you want your home page to say, time to hunt and peck, and patience.

This chapter tells you everything you need to make an adequate start. And if you get stuck, have the kids in your class help you out. If you are completely baffled, go to the Web site on the Internet to put your information in code for you. It will take a couple of days for you to get the return copy, but if you are interested, see:

URL: http://www.wizard.com/~fifi/pagemake.html

 IN THE CLASSROOM:

How to build your own home page

Goal

To design, code, and upload a home page with your students for your class.

Rationale

You want the World (Web) to know what you are doing, and a home page is your window to the world: Your class looks out, and the world looks in. You also want to reinforce skills in reading, writing, drawing, proofreading, and collaborating. And instruct in the new skill of programming.

Objectives

Compose a message on your home page that is meaningful. It represents your class to people who will meet you through the Internet. Develop expertise in collecting, organizing, and writing data (both textual and graphical), in using HTML, and in producing and maintaining a home page with selected links. Devise strategies for working together.

Procedures

- Designing your own home page is an excellent project for your class (or school) after everyone interested has been online for a while. When your students know a little about surfing and the types of information on the Web, they will probably have ideas for their own home page(s).

- Set the stage by telling your class that they can develop a short home page and put in on *Classroom Connect's* server. *Classroom Connect* requires pages that have a clear message and a reasonable purpose for using the space — the more focused, the better, and the more imaginative, the better. The focus of *Classroom Connect* is to help teachers harness the power of the Internet, so they provide many services for teachers. Check out their Web site at:

    URL: http://www.classroom.net/

- Brainstorm with your students to come up with the best reason for having a home page and a message for your class. One fourth-grade class has an interactive creative writing project, and the class is now communicating with people all over the world. Another class is doing a global weather survey. Yet another is communicating the results of a scientific experiment being done in several classrooms across the United States, the United Kingdom, and New Zealand. Only the imagination of you and your students constrains the boundaries.

- Spark your students' interest by having them find several good examples of home pages written by classes that are similar to yours in terms of grade level or subject, and see what your electronic neighbors have been doing. Talk about what makes an excellent home page, a so-so home page, and a not-so-good home page. Look for home pages that are elegant yet simple, that show a range of information links from simple to complex, and that have a clear and appealing purpose and message.

- Brainstorm with your class what they would like to see on their own home page. Revisit the issue of what your class's reason for having a home page and message ought to be. Generate a list of ideas for the content. Here's a starter list:

  - *Student stories*

  - *Interactive stories (stories written online in concert with other kids in other places)*

  - *Your class or school newspaper (you may want to include the class news digest that you are developing according to chapter 10)*

  - *Pictures drawn by students*

  - *Collaborative projects with other classes at your school or with other schools*

  - *A list of your email addresses and an invitation to keypals*

  - *Biographical sketches of your class*

  - *Favorite areas of study and hobbies with individual comments and questions*

  - *Science projects*

  - *Information and news about where you live, and maybe a virtual tour about the notable and scenic spots in your locality (like the one suggested at the end of chapter 12)*

- *Pictures of everything you talk about*
- *Audio clips and video footage (if you have the technical capacity)*
- *And oh! so much more*

When you publish your own and your students' email addresses to the world, realize that you are inviting yourself to be flooded with messages. Make sure you are prepared for the traffic. If you are ambitious, lead your class to become the force that organizes a home page for your entire school. (In that case, your class home page will be a link on the school Web site.) To involve other classes and even the principal means your class will assume the responsibility of teaching other people about the Internet. Think about the implications of this undertaking and talk it over thoroughly with all the major players. This can be a big project.

- After the brainstorming, set priorities. Develop an outline of your proposed home page before you start writing, and long before you start coding it. Without this outline, you may lose direction and focus, and end with a hodge-podge page that visitors will visit once but never again. Remind everyone that the page is going to be on the World Wide Web. This means that it will be viewed and read by possibly thousands of people all over the world who will build their only impression of you and your interests by reading your class home page. Posting a home page via the Web to the world is awesome, and is not, as our kids will agree, a responsibility to be taken lightly.

- Display the outline on a bulletin board in your room. On this display, establish a schedule of deadlines: dates when text has to be completed, when links have to be identified and coded, when the home page will have its test run, when it will be reviewed and modified, and when links have to be updated or maintained.

- Assign different parts of the project to different groups of students according to their stated interests. Allow everyone to work with as many different parts of the project — organization, text, coding, graphics, proofing, etc. — as they like, so that they can exercise their talents and skills and take ownership of the finished product. Here's a check list of some of the groups you'll probably need:

  - *Project coordinator (to help you keep up with everybody else)*
  - *Information and image gatherers*

- *Copywriters*
- *Coders*
- *Editors*
- *Proofreaders*
- *Maintenance staff*
- *Page designers and layout artists*
- *Artists and graphics designers*
- *Reporters (to get stories from other classes, the principal, parents)*
- *Webmaster(s)*

- You will need a group to talk with the people in charge of your intended server, whether your own school's systems technicians, a private server, a near-by university, a regional freenet, or some other on-ramp to the Information Superhighway. The job of this group is to establish your right to upload and the protocol for uploading your home page on their server.

- The group that maintains the computer files during the building process exercises critical hands-on responsibility. Not only must they manage the files of the various elements of your home page but also they need to keep a detailed list of all the files, with complete reference to titles and what each title means. This is work for your detail-minded students.

  For example, on my first Web site, I posted 105 separate files, each one with a different name. To remember what the file names represent, I made a master list of the file names and what is in each file. Sure, I can look in the file to determine what is in it, but a hard copy list is easier for me to refer to. Because I share Webmaster duties with another faculty member, we would be working at cross-purposes if we did not have our master list of files. Home pages have to be maintained and updated, and it is difficult to remember what 105 obscure abbreviations mean six months after they have been written, especially if they have been created by a number of students.

- While your students are engaged in all these many activities, even if your kids are mature and responsible, you will need eight arms and about the same number of eyes to keep up with all the groups and keep them focused on their tasks. Needless to say, no matter how young or old your students are, or how responsible and mature, you are the ultimate Webmaster and the buck stops with you.

- After the home page is up and running, you will need a hands-on Webmaster, an individual who is responsible in every way for every aspect of an active home page. That person will assuredly and ultimately, I repeat, be you. It would, however, be good developmental instruction for the students to choose the right person from their midst to be the student Webmaster of public record, your associate in this responsibility. Your Webmaster can have as many assistant Webmasters as seems desirable. I suggest rotating the job of Webmaster among the students who are competent to do the work; that way, more people can learn from the experience.

- Your students need to know that the class home page is not a passing fad but a high-stakes project that they are going to stick with through the entire year. I suggest, if possible, that you put a counter on your home page that keeps a record of "hits" — the number of times your home page has been visited. Seeing those hits accumulate will help maintain student interest. If you get enough hits, you might even sell advertising space on your home page.

- Another good way to maintain class interest is to program in email addresses into your home page, so that visitors can write to all of you. The address of the Webmaster needs to be there, of course, and don't forget to put student addresses on a file that links to your home page. Every student in your class ought to have his or her own email address, and it ought to link to your Web site. When children are born, they get Social Security numbers. Now, when they come of age to be "netizens" of the WWW, they get email addresses.

Technical production of your home page

After the home page copy has been composed, and the pictures and other information are gathered and organized, the home page needs to be formatted to be readable by a browser. You will need to teach your students how to put pictures in a correct format for uploading, how to write text files using the word processor, and how to code in HTML. None of this is as difficult as it may sound; the processes are simple ones. The kids who do this work, however, need to be the ones who take instruction well, who have an eye for detail, and who can follow directions.

If you are using a word processing program such as Microsoft Word or WordPerfect, click on *Save As* every time you want to save a document for uploading to your home page. Because the *Save As* function enables you to save files in a variety of formats, choose "text" or "ASCII text," and then click on *OK*. Your document is thereby saved as a machine-readable text file. Should you happen to forget and not save a document as a text file, it cannot be read on the Web. In addition, your browser will **not** be able to read any text file unless its name ends with the suffix *.html* (for Macintosh users) or *.htm* (for PC users). Therefore, a typical text file name might be "egc.html" and a typical image file name might be "egc.gif". The suffix ".html" has the function of telling the browser that the file is written in mark-up language, while the suffix ".gif" tells the browser that the file contains an image. The newest versions of some word processing programs now allow you to "Save As" an HTML file. This is a real time saver.

After a document has been word-processed and saved as a text file, put your proofreaders to work. Have them check for errors in content as well as spelling and grammar. You may want to have two groups of proofreaders, one for content and organization, another for spelling and grammar. When they have finished proofing a file, make sure that it is saved as a text file once again. You can change text in a document after it has been marked up. You'll find it much easier to make changes while the document is still a simple word-processing file, before it has been coded.

Your artists and coders need to work closely together. The artists help to design the page, while the coding crew puts in the tags to the text files. You will need to show your artists how to make image files using "gif," "jpeg," or "mpeg," format.

Your coders will need to learn how to code in HyperText Mark-up Language. Several HTML primers are available, and most of them are easy to understand. At the beginning of the chapter, eight HTML guides were listed. I've found quite a few other good HTML guides on the Net, so I listed a few more on the following page.

Beginner's Guide to HTML	http://www.ncsa.uiuc.edu/General/Internet/WWW/ HTMLPrimer.html
Beginner's Guide to URLs	http://www.ncsa.uiuc.edu/demoweb/url-primer.html
Crash Course on HTML	http://www.pcweek.com/eamonn/crash_course.html
GNN Select Internet: HTML	http://gnn.com/gnn/wic/wics/internet.html.html
Guide to HTML Commands	http://www.woodhill.co.uk/html/html.htm
HTML Quick Reference	http://www.cc.ukans.edu/info/HTML_quick.html
HTML: Working & Background	http://www.w3.org/pub/WWW/MarkUp/ MarkUp.html
Learning About HTML	http://www.indiana.edu/ip/ip_support/ learn_html.html
Project Cool Basic HTML	http://www.projectcool.com/developer/ framed-index.html

Choose the guide that is best for your coders and for yourself. If you do have a good group of direction-followers who can read documents, make sense of them, and put the directions to use, they should be able to work with any of the above documents on HTML. HTML is not a difficult language or code to learn, but you need to learn it so that you can talk with your HTML class experts. You cannot leave this task to your coders alone; they will need your assistance, especially the first time they start to code. I will offer a few basics on HTML, but to get you started, you need to consult the sources above.

When you are finished putting in all the tags, put the page through a trial run in your browser program. In Netscape you do this by going to the *Open New File* in the *File* pull-down menu. A window will appear asking where the new file is found. You locate that file, click on *Add*, then *Done*, then *OK*. Soon the Netscape screen will show off the document. If it has been coded correctly, it should look just as you want it to look. If it does not look that way, identify the errors and go back to the drawing board. Sometimes you will have to make many small changes in order for a file to look as you think it should look. (I've made about two perfect files in all the time I've been doing HTML — it's harder to get them perfect the first time around than you think.)

Home pages require a lot of feeding, watering, and tending; therefore, your maintenance group, including your Webmaster(s), will become more important over the long term. There are times when you do not have the time to do the needed maintenance on your home page. When, however, the information on a home page becomes dated and incorrect, you are definitely no longer putting our best foot forward! Look at the bottom of many Web sites and you will probably see a date. This date tells you the last time the page was updated. This is important if you are trying to get the most recent information. If you have date-sensitive information or links on your home page, you will feel the need for timely maintenance even more — possibly on a weekly or even daily basis. (I'm not exaggerating! Some Web sites are updated every day. My home page gets updated once a semester.) If, for example, your home page talks about a big event that's going to happen in the spring, and now it's already late summer and heading into fall, your home page needs maintenance.

Evaluation

The finished home page with an address on the Web is but one piece of evidence that the project was successful — the public component. Less obvious, but more important, are the skills that have been communicated and practiced: group participation, cooperation, and collaboration; reading, writing, drawing, layout design, proofreading, spelling and coding skills; the ability to follow directions; the honing of attention to detail; and the personal responsibility required to achieve presentable work for public display. Your class will have the opportunities to learn and participate every aspect of the curriculum. Putting a home page on the Web gives new meaning to the phrase "across the curriculum."

HTML Basics

At the beginning of this chapter, you saw some HTML coding — the A for anchor, <>, the /, and HREF=. There are several more and most of them are alliterative in nature, e.g., "HR" stands for horizontal rule. Users do not see any of these codes or tags when viewing your home page — unless they ask the browser to reveal the source code.

The page or document you want to code has four sections: Document Type, Header, Title, and Body. The document type is <HTML> and is placed at the beginning of the document or file. When you are finished with the document or file, you write </HTML>.

The title is the name of the document as it is going to show up on the browser window. It is written <TITLE> and at the end of the title, </TITLE>. The header <HEAD> is where the title is placed, and it ends with </HEAD>. Lastly comes the Body of the file or document, the bulk of the page. It is coded <BODY> and </BODY>.

Explanation	Code	Where to put it
Document Type	<HTML> </HTML>	beginning and end of file
Header	<HEAD> </HEAD>	descriptive information such as the title
Title	<TITLE> </TITLE>	must be within <head>
Body	<BODY> </BODY>	the majority of the document or file

Here's an example:

```
<html>
<head> <!-- HEADER --!>
<title>What's It All About, Anyway?</title>
</head>
<body> <!-- BODY --!>
</body>
</html>
```

HTML is not case sensitive. You may use upper-case letters, or lower-case letters, when you are composing tags (although I suggest being consistent). What you must not do is forget the <> or / marks. If even one > mark is left off, the tag will not be read correctly, and the document will not appear as you want it to appear. Watching for paired sets of bookends is one way that your proofreaders will prove their diligence.

Sample HTML

The phrase "The Information Superhighway" is coded several different ways below. Look at the tags, and see how the print changes.

Command	Coding	Result
Bold	The Information Superhighway	**The Information Superhighway**
Italics	<i>The Information Superhighway</i>	*The Information Superhighway*
Bold, Italics (together)	The Information Superhighway	***The Information Superhighway***
Centered	<center>The Information Superhighway</center>	The Information Superhighway

If you get the general idea, then you are ready for some more complicated coding. Use
 (line break) at the end of a line when you want a single carriage return. Use <p> when you want a double carriage return at the end of a paragraph and use <hr> to put in a horizontal rule or line across a document. Here are three tags or codes that do not need the </> tag or the other bookend. Here are some examples.

Code	What You Write
Line break	She likes to sing. He likes to dance
Paragraph break	She likes to sing.<p> He likes to dance.<p>
Horizontal Rule	<hr>

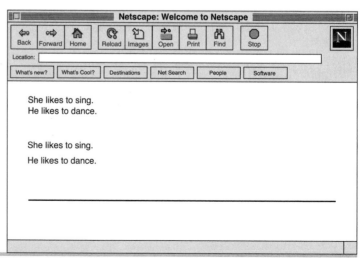

Creating Lists

To make lists, use either <ul></ul> (unordered list) or <ol></ol> (ordered list) tags along with <li> (link) tag. An unordered list is not numbered, where an ordered list is numbered 1, 2, 3, etc.

Here's an example using the <hr>, <br>, <ul> and <p> tags:

HTML Code

```
<hr><p>
We saw these animals:
<ul>
<li>goats
<li>pigs
<li>cows
</ul><p>
<hr>
```

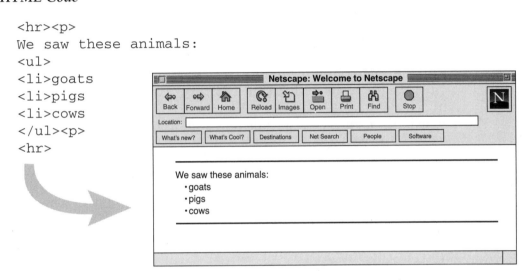

Here's the same example using a numbered list:

HTML Code

```
<hr><p>
We saw these animals:
<ol>
<li>goats
<li>pigs
<li>cows
</ol><p>
<hr>
```

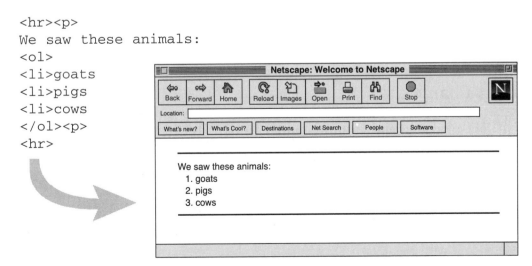

Hypertext Links

There's more. You want to connect your page to other pages, so you need to create hypertext links. Those are the underlines you see on Web pages that allow you to bounce from one page to another. There is a specific protocol for them. Remember reading this at the beginning of the chapter? Every time you want to create a link, you must anchor it in the main body of the text. Since "anchor" starts with "a" the tag starts out with an "<a" and a twist. Next, you want to refer to that other Web site. All Web sites have addresses or URLs, so you type in the URL. Here is a sample that will take a visitor to the Smithsonian Institution.

```
<a href="http://www.si.edu/resource/start.htm">
            The Smithsonian Institution</a>
```

If you typed this in an HTML document, it will look something like the following: The Smithsonian Institution, and, if it was coded correctly, by clicking on the underlined phrase, your visitor will be viewing one of the Web pages for the Smithsonian Institution in Washington, D.C.

The code is easy to remember. It starts with:

```
<a (for anchor)
<a href= (hypertext link to another URL)
<a href="http://address of document"
   (put in the URL for the new document)
<a href="http://address of document"> (end of tag)
<a href="http://address of document">Wonderful Document
   (title of the URL)
<a href="http://address of document">Wonderful Document</a>
   (ending anchor tag)
```

Font Changes

The type sizes and fonts are quite limited in HTML, so you'll have to be clever in their use to give your home page its own special look. The six type sizes available for headings and sub-heads in HTML, range from <h1>, the largest, to <h6>, the smallest.

HTML Code

```
<h1>MAIN TITLE</h1>
<h2>SMALL TITLE<h2>
<h3>SUB-HEAD</h3>
<h4>SUB-SUB-HEAD</h4>
<h5>SUB-SUB-SUB-HEAD</h5>
<h6>THE SMALL PRINT</h6>
```

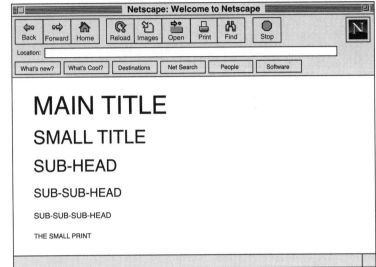

Be forewarned that some browsers cannot read h5 or h6 because they are too small. Netscape, however, can read these tags. As a helper, keep this reference chart handy!

Style	Pneumonic	Code
Bold	Bold	<b></b>
Italics	Italics	<i> </i>
Large Print	1	<H1></H1>
Small Print	6	<H6></H6>
Other Print Sizes	2 (larger than 3)	<H2></H2>
	3	<H3></H3>
	4	<H4></H4>
	5 (larger than 6)	<H5></H5>
Center	Center	<center></center>
Unordered list	list without numbers	<ul> </ul> (<li> needed in front of each item)
Ordered list	list with numbers	<ol> </ol> (<li> needed in front of each item)

HTML Editing Software

HTML can be fun, but there are other options than brute force coding. You can "borrow" code from Web sites; you can use an HTML generator that can be downloaded from the Internet, or you could buy an HTML generator such as Adobe PageMill. The HTML generators will automatically put in the tags where they are needed. The earlier programs were bulky, but newer programs, like PageMill, are not difficult to use. In addition, some of the newer word processing programs have HTML generators too. If you would like to download some HTML programs, visit some of the following Web sites.

HTML Writer — How to Get a Copy (Mac or Windows)	http://lal.cs.byu.edu/people/nosack/get_copy.html
HTML Assistant	http://www.w3.org/pub/WWW/Tools/html-assistant.html
HoTMetaL for free	http://www.sq.com/products/hotmetal/hm-ftp.htm
HTML Editor (for Mac)	http://www.w3.org/pub/WWW/Tools/HTML-editor.html
WWW HTML and Authoring Tools (this is a directory of many Web sites)	http://www.w3.org/pub/WWW/Tools/Overview.html
Yahoo List of HTML Converters, both Shareware and Freeware (this is a long directory)	http://www.yahoo.com/Computers_and_Internet/Internet/World_Wide_Web/HTML_Converters/Shareware_Freeware/

Lastly, I recommend that you check out the following site for more information in case you feel you need it: HTML Developer's JumpStation on the Web — http://oneworld.wa.com/htmldev/devpage/dev-page.html. I already listed HTML Quick Reference Guide earlier, but it is a good one. Check it out at http://www.cc.ukans.edu/info/HTML_quick.html. These well-organized Web sites are collections of tools, guides, articles, and techniques used on the Web.

Borrowing code

Just a few sentences ago, I mentioned that there are several ways to "get" code. One of the easiest ways to see how a Web page looks in HTML is to reveal it in HTML source code. Remember the *View / Document Source* in the pull-down menu

I talked about earlier? Now that you have some background with what HTML looks like, this direction might make more sense now. Study the codes that are embedded in the text to see how they make a Web page look. A few simple Web sites are listed below. Check them out to get a first-hand look at HTML. If you see something that you like, copy it and use that idea on your home page. (I did a lot of this for the first few files I developed.)

The Theory of Multiple Intelligences	http://k12.cnidr.org:90/edref.mi.intro.html
BCK2SKOL	http://web.csd.sc.edu/bck2skol/fall/fall.html
A very simple Web site I designed for a presentation about newspapers	http://www.csuchico.edu/educ/fun.html

Your home page can be simple or sophisticated. Start with easy stuff, and then as you and your class build confidence and skill, blast off from there. It may seem slow at first, but the new use of an ability always is tedious at the beginning. Don't be afraid to try new things — no point in being boring! By the way, I learned HTML and developed the Web site for my department in three weeks. It is possible!

How to publish your own home page

To publish pages on the Internet, you will submit your pages to a server computer using server software. The first thing to do is find out who is willing to publish your home page. If you are part of a freenet or school system that has home page space available, find out their requirements and start coding away. You can also have two home pages published free by *Classroom Connect*.

URL: http://www.classroom.net/classweb

You can search the Web using the command "free Web space" to find other places that will publish your Web page for free (or at least inexpensively). I just did a search with MetaCrawler and came back with 28 hits. There is a lot of Web space, so there is no excuse not to publish your page.

Things you don't want to do

I would be remiss if I did not mention some of my pet peeves about home page construction. I'm sure you have seen Web pages that are just too busy, have a background color that looks terrible, or have just too much stuff on them. Think about those things that really bother you when you visit a Web site, and try not to make those mistakes. Here are few of the design problems that really bother me.

1. Frames. Netscape now supports frames (and I wish it didn't). They look interesting, but if you want to copy or print anything from a page that is "framed" you can't. You can't bookmark these pages, nor can you use the "back" command.

2. Scrolling texts, marquees, and constantly running animations. I find these pages very distracting. A Web site with moving images on it makes me want to click to another site fast. I use the Web to find information, not to see Times Square.

3. Complex URLs. You know what I mean . . . the URLs that seem to go on forever and ever. URLs have to be typed perfectly, so the chances of making a typo are greater with a long or complex list of meaningless letters than with a short list of sensible abbreviations. Try to use short names with all lower-case characters and no special characters such as # or $.

4. Really long download times. Sites that have lots of graphics or exceptionally large audio/video files take too long to download, especially in a school setting. If it takes too long to get the information, my students become bored. You don't need that!

5. Outdated information. I hate it when a Web site disappears and there is no forwarding address!

6. Long scrolling pages. Somewhere I read that only 10 percent of all users scroll beyond the information that is visible on the screen when the page comes up. That's why I like critical content and navigation options on the top part of the page.

7. Blinking pages. Last, but not least, I cannot stand pages that blink at me. At first I thought they were fun, and I made a few. But as I see more of them out there on the Web, I'm sorry I ever liked them at all. I find them annoying, especially if I'm trying to read something near the blinking. Blinks would be OK if the user could turn them off!

HTML tutorial

To test your mastery of HTML, you can take the tutorial developed by Eric Meyer at Case Western Reserve University. Turn on your browser and open:

URL: http://www.cwru.edu/help/introHTML/toc.html

(By the way, when you are done with the tutorial, send him your comments. He will appreciate it.)

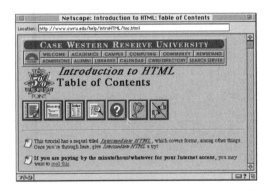

Whether or not your class gets a home page up and running, send me some email about what you are doing with the Internet. You can reach me at URL: mailto:ecotton@oavax.csuchico.edu. Tell me about what your students are doing on the Internet.

Notes

_____

_____

_____

_____

_____

_____

_____

Chapter 6

Advanced Web

Advanced Web. It sounds like we are going to learn how to become better spiders. In many ways, that's what this chapter is all about. There are many enhancements being developed to make the Web easier to travel. Because of these advances in technology, the Web is more colorful, more musical, and more interactive than ever before.

Given the nature of the ever-changing Internet, enhancements are made nearly everyday. I'm only going to discuss a few of the major advancements, such as HTML (colors, backgrounds, and tables); and multimedia on the Internet (audio, video, chat, VRML, Java, and a host of plug-ins). Multimedia and plug-ins are in their infancy, but both have certainly come a long way from the meager beginnings of Web in 1992! Keep an eye on these two Internet features, because that's where the action is now.

Web site design

Okay, you're ready to add a little life to your Web sites. You've seen the Web sites with ugly colors and busy backgrounds. You probably wondered, "Why would anybody do that to their Web site?" I've wondered the same thing, and like my mother used to say, "Beauty is in the eye of the beholder." What is beautiful to you is not always beautiful to someone else.

A good Web site has a home page (the first page or main menu) with all the important information seen in the first screen. When you open a home page and see nothing and you have to wait for a graphic to appear, you are probably going to move on to another site as soon as possible. Keeping your initial Web page simple is the key.

A good Web site should not be too busy. Remember when friends got their first computers that used different fonts? You probably got letters from them that were written in 17 different fonts. After awhile, the fun wore off, and they wrote the letters in one font. The same is true for Web sites: Don't go overboard. While variety might be the spice of life, it can be distracting. It's another way to discourage people from visiting your Web site. After all, if you are creating an information bank for your students, you want them to visit your Web site, stay there, learn something, then come back again and again.

Look at some commercial Web sites. See how they have used color, fonts, and logos. Their sites are usually clean and load quickly. Take your cue from them. Usually, their logo is small, less than 20k in size. The colors are attractive, not offensive. You get to the meat of the document quickly on the first screen. If you have a logo, don't make it so big that it takes up a whole screen. That means two things: a long download time (which is boring), and the logo is taking up valuable space that can be used for information.

You want to design your document with these simple rules in mind.

- Organize your information so it is easy to retrieve; that means tables and frames. There are lots of good Web sites out there that tell you how to add them to your site. Reading some of these directions is like wading through molasses. I let my students show me how to work with them first, then I follow their lead. The kids have the time to play with different Web sites and tags, and they "get it" better than most of us oldsters can. My first rule of thumb is to look at what is out there. If I see a table I like, I look at the source code (by selecting View Document Source under the View menu in Netscape) and copy away! I put my material into their table and it usually works. After I've done that for a couple of pages, I begin to see the logic of the tags and I can figure it out from there.

If you are interested in working with tables, and frames, here are a few sites that will be of use.

The Down and Dirty Handbook of HTML
   URL: http://metro.turnpike.net/D/DanMM/howhtml.htm

This site gives some good ideas about tables and frames.

The Web Designer
   URL: http://web.canlink.com/
      webdesign/

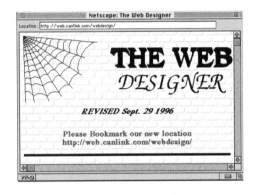

It offers lots of user friendly comments about design, tables, frames, animated graphics, and the like. It's a good place to look at if you want to become a proficient coder.

Project Cool
   URL: http://www.projectcool.com/developer/

This site features ideas about tables, frames, etc.

I like tables. They help organize information in a matrix. If you don't think in a matrical fashion, stay away from tables. Frames, which are not available on all browsers, is another issue. If you are using Netscape or another "frames ready" browser you can at first grasp the organizational scheme, then the problem, of frames. They divide the screen into two or more independent areas so you can have two "things" happening on your Web page at the same time. This is kind of cool. However, if you want to click back to an item on a previous framed page, you have to press down your mouse button and hold it, then select Back from a menu that pops up. Intuitive? Hardly! [Note: The latest versions of Netscape (3.0 and higher) allow you to click backwards more easily in frames.] Thus, if you use frames, you basically disable the all-important Back button on most older browsers. Is that something you want to do?

Another little touch many people like to add to their Web sites is a counter. You know, the little set of numbers that say how many times people visit your Web site? They are a double-edged sword! What happens if your class builds the quintessential Web site with a counter and no one shows up to visit? Is it your job to access that site a hundred times just to make your kids feel better? But good publicity (and there's lots of ways to publicize your site) will probably garner a few hits.

While we are in the area of making the Web site more attractive, don't forget color. You can add backgrounds that are plain or textured. You can change the color of your leading links and your followed links as well as the color of the font (but realize that some browsers will then make the text nearly illegible if you do this). To see how to add more color to your Web site, look at this list of URLs. Every one of them is easy to understand.

The Style Guide to HTML

URL: http://www.w3.org/pub/WWW/Provider/Style/Overview.html

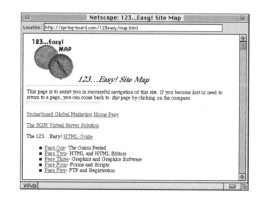

Easy, 1, 2, 3

URL: http://spring-board.com/123easy/map.html

Check out the background and graphics links.

Creating Basic Web Pages

URL: http://www.dcn.davis.ca.us/ ~csandvig/ip/pccourse.htm

Here is another good place to look for color, graphics, and backgrounds. You can also search the Web for sites by asking for "HTML backgrounds." You will be surprised at all the hits that are returned.

Now the Real Bells, Whistles — and Third Dimension, Too!

In the last six months, the Web has taken on a new dimension — that of multimedia. Simply put, multimedia is the "plug-ins" (as they are often called) that make a plain Web site explode with sound, color, added dimension, or all three.

Right now, most multimedia is not aimed at the education market, so it's difficult to find multimedia Web sites that have what I call a "curricular" value. Given that, multimedia Web sites do have splash!

Here's a great example:

> *MayaQuest Home Page*
>   URL: http://www.mecc.com/mayaquest.html

Click on the "shocked" link. To hear the music of the trek through ancient Mayan ruins in Central America. Puzzle pieces float on the screen and slowly link to form a textured tablet that has four buttons on it. Click on the buttons and they light up and transport you to the link of your choice. It really is interesting to look at. Does it enhance 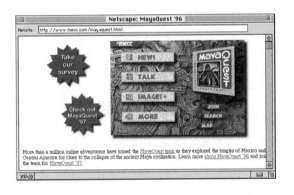 the Web site? Is it worth the download time? Subsequent pages are not "shocked" (thank goodness, as the download time would be too long). "Shock" in this case is shorthand for "Shockwave" which is a plug-in to Netscape that integrates sound, animation, and video together.

If you are interested in seeing the MayaQuest "Shocked" Web site and you don't have the plug-in, you can download it right there. The directions for downloading and installing it in Netscape 2.0 or higher will be the next screen you see on the site.

Macromedia Support: Shockwave

URL: http://www.macromedia.com/support/technotes/shockwave/index.html

Another Web site that uses Shockwave is . . .

Planet Hawaii

URL: http://planet-hawaii.com/production/shock/ph/

Only the first page is "shocked," but you get a good idea of what this plug-in can do. It takes over two minutes for a 14.4 modem to download the sound and animation for this page, and it takes less than 30 seconds for the effect to play itself out.

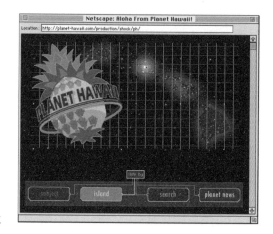

The Shockwave plug-in is well worth downloading and installing in your Internet browser. But it's only the beginning!

Virtual Reality (VRML) is another exciting multimedia phenomenon on the Internet. VRML is a programming language Web designers use to place Virtual Reality scenes and walk-throughs on their Web pages. You can download various VRML plug-ins and players into your Web Browser. Once these VRML scenes or animations are loaded into your browser through these plug-ins, they can give your screen an arcade game appearance with three-dimensional depth and animated graphics. One of the best Web sites to look at for Virtual Reality in action is "Stonehenge." If you want to see Stonehenge, you must have a fast Windows-based computer (a 100 megahertz Pentium or faster is recommended — yikes!), as the Web site is designed for Windows 3.1 or Windows95. There are, however, VRML plug-in emulators that let you view this site with a Macintosh computer.

Stonehenge

> URL: http://www.superscape.com/intel/shenge.htm

This Web site is phenomenal but it took me 12 minutes to download with my 14.4 modem. All the while I was thinking, "What are my kids going to do if they have to wait this long?"

Once the scene is loaded, you are presented with a view of Stonehenge, at dawn on the day of the Summer Solstice. You see the sun rising slowly above the circle of stones. You can walk around the huge liths, experience the past, and glimpse into the future. It is completely interactive and even interesting for Mac users without the plug-in.

For those of us who are still bewildered by plug-ins and what they mean, you can get even more bewildered by this site:

Falken's Maze

> URL: http://cybertools.thru.net/ tools.shtml

This Web site tries to organize all the plug-ins out there and tell you what they do. Open this URL to find out what it's all about.

Try GNN for a write up on plug-ins. It tends to be written in an English I can understand some of the time.

GNN

> URL: http://webcrawler.com/ select/internet.browsers.html

At the Mac Plug-in Center you can find out information about the different plug-ins that are available for the Macintosh, and you can download the plug-ins you want.

Mac Plug-in Center

URL: http://wso.williams.edu/~jsolomon/plugins.html

A similar page for Windows folks is this Web site:

Browserwatch

URL: http://browserwatch.iworld.com

My university also has a site on plug-ins that I found useful probably because I know the people who wrote the site.

California State University, Chico

URL: http://www.csuchico.edu/computing/INTERNET/helpers.html

If you want even more information on plug-ins, do a search in MetaCrawler. In the query box type plug-ins and you will be surprised at how many links are returned.

The next step is putting or "embedding" plug-ins into your Web site. That is an art unto and of itself, and one I have not yet mastered. I'm still reading information on how to do this.

Live Update Page

URL: http://www.liveupdate.com/embed.html

You can learn how to write the scripts needed for plug-ins to work at this site. This is definitely in the realm of advanced Web design, and I'm not there yet. (My kids probably are!)

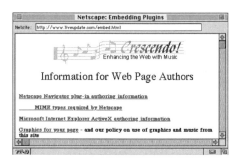

Chat

Chat has been around for a while in the form of Internet Relay Chat or IRC. I believe it has now finally come of age. There are many Web sites now that offer online chat lines for teachers and chat lines for students. Last year, that was not the case.

I like Chat! I think this is a welcome addition to the Internet. It makes the Net more interactive, more real, more "now oriented." With Chat, I can talk to folks in real time, unlike the talking I do when using a email program.

The other day, I had a Chat with four other people. We were all talking about this book, getting some of the essentials squared away. I could chat with the publisher, the editor, the illustrator, and the programmer about *The Online Classroom*. Not only was it fun, we were able to answer some questions that had been eluding us. I have also used this same function to talk over articles with three of my colleagues from three different institutions. Since all of us teach at different universities across the U.S., the phone bill would have been prohibitive for the hour that we were on the line. To make matters even better, at the end, we all had a script of what we said that we could refer to for future guidance and clarity. That is not possible with a telephone conversation.

There are several Chat plug-ins available for Web users. Right now I am using the Global Chat plug-in for my Internet class.

Global Chat
   URL: http://arachnid.qdeck.com/chat/schedule.html

At this site, you can also download a free copy of the program.

Chat lines, in their various forms, have great potential in a classroom. Look into MUDs (Multi-User Dungeons) and MOOs (Multi-User Dungeon, Object Oriented) if you have telnet software, as well as IRCs and the other chat lines that are out there. With a chat line you can talk to folks (by typing on your keyboard), in real time, about a particular issue, or project. You can exchange ideas quickly as well as get your own point of view across to others. I've read of an astronaut giving a first-person account of a Space Shuttle flight to a group of folks in a classroom hundreds of miles away. Can you imagine what it feels like to "talk" to an astronaut, ask him or her questions, and then get the responses from space? What a powerful tool!

As the technology matures, chat programs will become better forums for the exchange of ideas. Already, Quarterdeck, the developer of Global Chat, has created an Internet counterpart to a live long distance telephone call. With the correct software and a microphone, you can actually talk to someone else (who also has the proper software and telephone) over the Internet. Call this an Internet phone or sorts. This can be a "long distance" telephone conversation over the Internet, for the price of the local dial-up phone call to the Internet provider. I wonder how long the various telephone companies are going to let this type of communication happen? Or at least when they'll try to force regulations on these nearly-free conversations in cyberspace.

There is a problem, however. Don't confuse Web chats on chat lines with Internet Relay Chat, or IRC. Web chats and chat lines are organized discussions about specific topics. IRCs seem to be "meet" markets where there may be questionable language and conversation among the participants. On the other hand, don't prejudge IRCs as all negative. Some interesting and educational channels have been known to pop up on IRC servers.

Video clips and CU-SeeMe

The Web doesn't contain just static text and pictures anymore. Many Web sites now have short video clips embedded in them. One click, and they download and begin running on your screen. Look for URLs that have *.mpeg*, *.qt* (QuickTime) or *.mov* written in them. For these URLs you need the correct plug-in to view their

movies within your browser. Again, check out the plug-in sites mentioned earlier so you can download the appropriate one. (You can take up a lot of disk space with plug-ins, something else to keep in mind.)

Video clips add a different perspective to a Web site. They might make a site more interesting or they might just be a novel gadget that is hot. Like all plug-ins right now, they take time to download, and once downloaded, they do not take much time to play through. I find that disappointing. I have talked to several Web programmers about multimedia and they agree that while plug-ins are fun, they seem to be found right now in the commercial sites, and educational sites are only using them at a basic level.

Here are a few movie plug-in sites:

QuickTime Movies
URL: http://www.MediaCity.com/~erweb/

Apple Computer, Inc.
URL: http://qtvr.quicktime.apple.com/

QuickTime Player
URL: http://qtvr.quicktime.apple.com/InMac.htm

Some Web sites make use of live video! I've seen sites that have a video camera aimed at a refrigerator and the viewer can see how many times the door is opened during the day. At my university, there was a camera aimed at a small parking lot. It takes a new picture of the parking lot every three minutes. Since my husband works in the building by that parking lot, I check on the site to see if there are any parking spaces available before I pick him up.

There are positive curricular uses for live video. I always hearken back to the bottom line — how can I use this tool with my curriculum? What is an objective for this Web site that will advance my curriculum? Looking at a Web site for the sake of a video on a refrigerator does not relate to the curriculum. This leads to CU-SeeMe (pronounced "see you, see me"), a program developed by the folks at

Cornell University. It allows Internauts to view each other in real-time provided that both users have video receiving and send units — basically, the free CU-SeeMe software and a video camera like a Connectix QuickCam ($100).

CU-SeeMe has been used by doctors in remote locations to clarify medical problems. There have been several Internet Conferences where attendees show up at a "studio" across the country that has a CU-SeeMe set-up. The attendees see and talk to each other via the Internet and video hook-up. It's the ultimate high-tech business meeting! A friend of mine uses CU-SeeMe to talk with his cousin who is a professor at another university. He says it's just like a phone call, but with live

pictures. Very cool! CU-SeeMe can be a powerful device to get two or more groups of folks talking about a common topic. To learn more, go to this site:

> *CU-SeeMe HQ*
>
> URL: http://cu-seeme.cornell.edu

Java

The recent talk on the Web has been about Java, yet another new programming language used to make changes to Web pages and their contents. If you are using Netscape 2.x you can access the most basic form of Java that's imbedded in Web pages — JavaScript. However, you need Netscape 3.x or higher to load Java applets that have been imbedded in Web pages. These small Java applets, which are actually small programs that run inside of Web pages, are the reason that everyone is so excited about it!

Java is still an infant programming language and is complicated, to say the least. Bruce Carter, the Division Head of the Instructional Development Division at Boise State University told me the following when I asked him to explain Java to me in simple language.

Java is a programming language that is gaining popularity on the Web due to its support of different computer platforms: multiplatform. You can write little

"applets" (miniature programs) in it and attach them to your Web pages. As to why it's important, well, right now it's a raging fad. I'm sure it will evolve into a more useful tool along with the Internet and Web in general. Right now, it's just something for Webheads to tinker with . . . Slightly different from Java is JavaScript, which is a scripting language that you can use right in your Web pages. Essentially the same description applies, though it's still evolving into something really useful.

I asked the same question to John Hart, another programming expert and he said this:

> "The source code [for Java] is compiled to run as an executable program on either the Web server side or on the browser side [applets]. Java can do a variety of things. As with most programming languages, it all depends on the author's intent; for instance, guestbooks, counters, and general forms handling, can be accomplished with Java. There are security concerns, especially for Java programs (applets) running on the client's machine, and the applets are limited to what they can perform on the client's machine."

For "more than you ever wanted to know" detailed information on Java and what it can do, go to:

Java FAQ
  URL: http://sunsite.unc.edu/javafaq/javafaq.html

Java White page
  URL:http://java.sun.com/doc/whitePaper.Platform/CreditsPage.doc.html

A Java tutorial (how to write Java applications and applets) can be found at:

Java Tutorial
  URL: http://java.sun.com/books/
    Series/Tutorial/index.html

Additional information and sources can be found at the JavaSoft (Sun Microsystems) site:

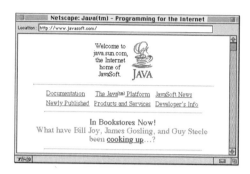

JavaSoft Home Page
URL:site: http://www.javasoft.com/

A nontechnical description can be found at:

Java Paper
URL: http://www.december.com/works/java.html

Watch for Java and JavaScript Web sites as more will be developed soon.

The Future of the Web

The Web is changing quickly. Simple Web sites will soon be enhanced with music, graphics, animated graphics, movies, and three dimensional images. I am not convinced that these are going to be helpful to classroom teachers as they stand now. Real time chat and video links to other people are already here. I am convinced they show promise in curriculum planning. Look into all of these enhancements as they are the harbingers of the future of teaching on the Internet.

Chapter 7

The Other Internet Tools

When the U. S. Department of Defense started the Internet (then called ARPANET) in the late '60s, they wanted to create a computer network so developers and researchers could easily communicate with each other using different types of computer systems. There was a real advantage to this type of compatibility across platforms.

This early network linked research universities, research laboratories, and some military labs together using communication programs such as telnet, ftp (file transfer protocol), and email. With telnet and ftp, a scientist could download files that were stored on computers anywhere in the U.S. Within a decade, the network grew to include connections in other countries, and telnet and ftp were standards of communication worldwide.

The network continued to grow and more demands were made on it. To meet these demands, gopher was created. Instead of telnetting to a site and ordering a file sight-unseen, as was the case with ftp, a user could now read the file at a gopher site. In addition, "ordinary" people were starting to access the network, and newsgroups were formed. At first the newsgroups revolved around topics related to the ftp archives, but as more lay people began using the network, the role of newsgroups expanded to include special interest forums in hundreds of areas. The Net now had users from more walks of life than ever before.

In 1991, Tim Berners-Lee, director of W3 Organization and an affiliate of CERN, created the World Wide Web using hypertext links. The World Wide Web was the force that brought about the current exponential use of the Internet. You didn't have to be a researcher or a scientist to use this communication device. Simplified navigation programs were developed; the old ARPANET ceased to exist. Almost overnight, millions of ordinary folks like you and me were accessing the Internet.

Internet tool evolution

As each decade brought a different type of user to the Internet, it also brought different types of demands on the system. As the users changed, the navigation programs needed to become easier and more user-friendly. Telnet and ftp are from that first generation of Internet programs. They were used by researchers and scientists with lots of computer savvy. However, easy for them, does not mean it is necessarily easy for all of us to use. Ftp is not very user-friendly, what with compressing and decompressing files, and burrowing through pathways and directories to find a particular file. Gopher was part of the next generation of navigation programs. It is easier to use than either telnet or ftp, but not nearly as powerful as current Web browser programs. This chapter will look at three dinosaurs of the Internet: telnet, ftp and gopher. Unlike dinosaurs, these navigation programs are not extinct yet, but I believe they will be in the near future as the new browsers become capable of doing a wider variety of more sophisticated tasks.

Telnet

We are used to working with icons and a mouse when on a computer. Telnet was created before either of those two inventions! The telnet software lets you login to a remote computer to get information from it. Once you are at that

computer, you use your keyboard and type commands telling that computer "out there" what information you want. Because telnet was invented before icons and "mice" were used, you can only use your keyboard for communication. For those of us who are used to clicking on buttons or pulling down menus, telnet can be a challenge since you cannot do any of those things. In addition, you have to be a good typist! If you type a URL incorrectly in your Web browser, you get an error message. In telnet, if you type something incorrectly, you get nothing, not even a message. And to make matters worse, on some machines you cannot even use the backspace key to erase!

Technically speaking, telnet transforms your computer into a front-end terminal that works off of a remote computer, much in the way that the computer at an ATM (bank machine) works off of the bigger, smarter computer inside the bank. Front-end computers tend to be "dumber" than the computers they work off of, and that will be the case with your computer: Your keyboard will work, but your mouse won't; and on your keyboard, the delete key will work only some of the time. Because telnet is letting your computer work with another computer, you will often need a password or other means of access to get inside.

As a result of this clunkiness, when I am using telnet I read all the prompts carefully, type deliberately, and try to remember the magic words that enable me to make up for the lack of a delete key and a mouse. That way, when I make a typo, I can rectify the problem with a minimum of fuss.

How to use telnet

To use telnet to connect to the Internet, do the following:

1. With your mouse, double click on the telnet icon to open the connection.

2. Wait for the beginning advertisement to clear from the screen, pull down the "file" menu, and select "open document." A dialogue box will appear that asks you to type in the session name or host.

3. Type in the address of the place you want and hit return. (Telnet calls this the Host/Session name.)

4. A menu will be displayed that will tell you the login or password you must use to access the system. It will also give you directions on how to erase mis-typed information and how to exit the site. Read and remember this information! You will need it later.

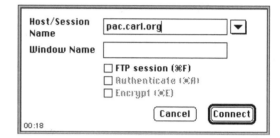

You have now established a telnet connection. Besides only being able to use the arrow keys, telnet has another quirk — it is case sensitive. That means, if the login requests some curious combination of UPPER and lower case letters, you must login with that precise combination of UPPER and lower case letters. Telnet allows neither creativity nor disagreement at the keyboard. If you do not login as requested, you will not get to that location.

I have found two reasons for using telnet: online libraries and searching through ftp archives. I think the libraries are more useful of the two, so I'll try to explain it first. It will all make sense, trust me. ; -)

Library access via telnet

The Internet gives a new meaning to the phrase "go to the library!" For fully online libraries, you'll find an electronic "card" catalogue of books, articles, reprints, etc. Some libraries, however, are not fully online, while a few have only part of their collection online — usually the more recent titles.

I use telnet for every library search I do. It is much easier for me to sit at my computer and find what I need than doing the same thing in the real library. Besides, I'm a night person who tends to want to do searches at midnight, and most libraries are not open at that time of night. To borrow the slogan from the Yellow Pages company, "Let your fingers do the walking."

The CARL Library System

One fabulous library system to visit is CARL (Colorado Alliance of Research Libraries). CARL is more than one library; it is a network of libraries around the world. When I lived on Guam, where library access was difficult, CARL was there. CARL and I have been friends for years! CARL gives access to current magazine articles, databases, university and public library systems, the whole ERIC database, and UnCover, which is a listing of journal and magazine articles and catalogues.

At many access points, CARL is free and open to the public; at some access points, CARL requires membership. (For example, some universities restrict use of CARL to faculty, staff, and students.) The means of gaining a CARL account, and the accompanying protocols, vary from server to server. However, there are some sites where you can browse the databases without an account and without accumulating any charges. The limitation is that you will not be able to download what you find. At other CARL sites you'll be able to make off like a bandit. The CARL site below is a pac or "public access site" so it is open to the Internet public. To telnet to CARL, do the following:

Open Connection

Host/Session: pac.carl.org (pac stands for Public Access Catalogue)

Login: pac

Now comes the tricky part. You are going to get a prompt asking you for the type of terminal you are using. You must respond with a terminal type, or telnet will quit. Many computers emulate a VT100 terminal, and that is option 5 on the telnet menu. If you are using a different kind of terminal, consult with your local techie. Select 5 and press return.

```
                        pac.carl.org
WELCOME TO CSI.CARL.ORG [PORT $ZTCO #23 WINDOW $ZT2.#PTZE67U]
TELSERV - T9553D30 - (17NOV95) - (IPMACA)


Available Services:

PAC      EXIT
Enter Choice> pac
Welcome to the CARL system
Please identify your terminal. Choices are:
1.ADM (all)
2.APPLE,IBM
3.TANDEM
4.TELE-914
5.VT100
6.WYSE 50
7.ZENTEC
8.HARDCOPY
9.IBM 316x
Use HARDCOPY if your terminal type isn't listed..
SELECT LINE #:
```

The next screen offers you a number of choices:

1. Library catalogs (including government publications)
2. Current article indexes and access (including UnCover and ERIC)
3. Information databases (including Encyclopedia)
4. Other Library systems
5. Library and System news.

Select the choice you want, and type in the number. Just keep on responding to the questions by typing in the correct answer at the prompt.

In addition to libraries, there are other telnet sites available. However, most of these sites are slowly moving over to the Web and are more readily accessible through a browser like Netscape or Internet Explorer. Listed below are some of the telnet sites that I've visited recently and found fruitful.

UmassK12

Host/Session: k12.ucs.umass.edu
Login: guest (use lower case letters)
also available at http://k12.oit.umass.edu

ERIC

Host/Session: ericir.syr.edu
Login: gopher
also available at http://ericir.syr.edu

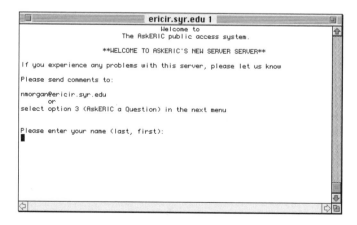

DCLOS (Dartmouth College Library Online System)
Host/Session: lib.dartmouth.edu
Login: (no login was required when I did it)
Exit Command: bye or quit

Big Sky
Host/Session: bigsky.bigsky.dillon.mt.us
login: bbs or visitor
Exit Command: bye

Each of these telnet sites will give you access to a library or database that might be useful to you or your curriculum. The UMassK12 site is for Massachusetts educators, but you can use the guest menu to find information about selected newsgroups and download some lesson plans and science experiments. They also have a mirror location on the Web. You can telnet to the ERIC database, also mirrored on the Web, to gain access to the wealth of information that the various ERIC clearinghouses provide.

At DCLOS you have access to the CIA World Factbook, the full text of some of Shakespeare's plays, an electronic dictionary, and if you are a faculty member, all of Robert Frost's poems. The Big Sky Telegraph in Dillon, Montana offers educational resources and classroom teaching ideas ranging from lesson plans to science labs. You have to subscribe to the service, but you can login as a visitor to check it out. Big Sky has a mirror site on the Web which is a lot more colorful and easier to use.

Big Sky mirror site
URL: http://macsky.bigsky.dillon.mt.us/

Ftp

Ftp stands for File Transfer Protocol and goes hand in hand with telnet. In the old days, you needed telnet to get to ftp. At the telnet prompt, you would type ftp and there it was. Times have changed. You can now access ftp without telnet, but it still does the same stuff it always did — accessing files from a computer out there in cyberspace and transferring those files to your computer. There are at least two types of ftp: anonymous and otherwise. We are going to talk about anonymous ftp because these sites are accessible by everyone. I only use one "otherwise" ftp and that is at my university when I have to download Web pages. That ftp is only available to Webmasters with the correct password.

At first, I was more unlucky than lucky with ftp, and if you have ever tried to download some files from an anonymous ftp site, you, too, may have turned away in frustration. It is getting easier because the new Web browsers will take you directly to ftp sites where you can download information quickly and easily. The old dedicated ftp programs will not do that!

Because ftp archives are cram-packed with software programs (freeware and shareware); electronic versions of books and manuscripts; hypercard stacks; clip art, audio and video clips; games; and just about everything else, you do need to know what to do with an anonymous ftp file. The best way to find and access ftp archives is by your browser, just by typing in *ftp://* and the URL at the location box, and away you go! Using my browser and an *ftp://* URL, I downloaded the most recent version of my printer driver, the most recent versions of Netscape and Internet Explorer, all the plug-ins I could ever want for my browsers, and as a diversion, a few games along the way.

Now is also a good time to warn you that ftp files are notorious carriers of computer viruses, so whenever you execute a file transfer, be sure to check for viruses before you install the program or upload the file on your computer. If you don't know how to check for viruses, holler for your techie friend again!

If, for some reason, you have a Fetch or ftp program on your computer, you might want to use it now, just for practice. Activate ftp by double-clicking on the icon. After the advertisement for ftp disappears, go to File in the pull-down menu and select Open ftp. At that point a dialogue box appears where you will type in the address you want.

Let's decode an ftp address so this will make some sense to you. The anonymous ftp for *PC Magazine* is ftp.cco.caltech.edu. Since *PC Magazine* is one of the most popular computer magazines in publication, why not get an online version of it.

Address:	ftp.cco.caltech.edu
User Name:	anonymous
Password:	(your email address)
path:	/pub/ibmpc/pcmag/

An ftp address looks similar to an email address without the @ sign. In this case, ftp tells the computer that you are going to a file transfer protocol; .cco is the name of the server where the file resides; .caltech is the location of the computer; and .edu is the domain of the server. The ftp archive for *PC Magazine* is at CalTech, an educational institution.

Next comes User Name — your name or the name you are using for this purpose. Since we are talking about anonymous ftp archives, your user name in this case is "anonymous." When the dialogue box asks for your password, type in your email address (or you can leave it blank). By typing in your address, you are telling the server who is accessing the computer site. Since you are going to be getting something for free, this is a polite thing to do.

When the dialogue box asks for the "path" you have two choices. You can either type in the whole thing or break it up into smaller parts. The quicker way of typing /pub/ibmpc/pcmag/ might work, but sometimes the ftp software gets cranky and it will just whirl around for hours!

The forward slashes (/) signal changes in directories or movement to a subsequent file. If you type a path one segment at a time it will look something like this: The path or directory you are seeking is /pub/ which stands for "public access." Click on it and you will see a list of files in alphabetical order. Scroll down that list until you see /imbpc/ and click on that. Another list of files will appear, and you scroll down that list until you see /pcmag/ (*PC Magazine*), the file you are looking for. Now double-click on /pcmag/ and then click on the issue you want to download.

Sounds easy, but wait! There's more to it!

Decompression/compression and ftp

There is one more aspect that I alluded to before, that of decompressing the file to make it readable. Once you have seen a list of ftp archives, you might have noticed they have little suffixes at the end of them. Suffixes that look like .txt, .tar, .hqx, or .zip are just a few examples. These suffixes can sometimes give you bad news. The only one I really like to see is .txt as that says the file I want to download is a text file that I can read without doing anything else. The other suffixes say the file has been compressed into a special format and for me to read it, I will have to decompress it. YUCK! Now you have to learn something else . . . the temperamental niceties of dealing with decompression software!

To get ftp to work to its potential you will need copies of different decompression programs (Mac folks need Stuffit Expander; PC folks need PKUNZIP or PUNZIP). It's lucky that the latest versions of browsers like Netscape and Internet Explorer have the appropriate decompression programs built into them. If you do not have a new browser, you can download a decompression program, buy one, or call your local, friendly compu-techie, who will get you the programs you need and tell you how to use them.

You need these decompression programs in order to read the file! When was the last time you wrote something extremely short (besides a grocery list)? I don't think I ever have! The same thing is true for files or archives in ftp. They are all long because they contain lots of information. This information takes up lots of space, and space on a computer is not easy to find. To alleviate the space problem, the first-generation researchers developed ways to compress the long files into shorter files. These researchers thought it was great fun to create a file, compress it down to almost nothing, then store it on an archive that other researchers could

access. The other researchers would find out about this great "little" archive, download it, and with their decompression software programs, they would stretch it back to its original size and read the information. Files that have been compressed cannot be read by mere humans . . . we need to stretch them back out to normal to read them, and this is why you need decompression software.

After you have downloaded an anonymous file, you need to check it for viruses, decompress it, then load it on your computer, all before you can read it or use it. That's just a few of the reasons why ftp is not user friendly. However, if you know an ftp location you'd like to visit, type ftp:// and the full address in the location box in your browser. Hit return. Your browser will start to download the file, decompress or unstuff it as needed, and leave it on your desktop for you to put through a virus check program before you install it on your computer. The current Web browsers have made the onerous task of file transfer almost bearable!

Archie and telnet

Before I took this little ftp birdwalk, I said there was one other use for telnet — that of searching and finding ftp archives. Just as you search the World Wide Web with Lycos, WebCrawler, InfoSeek, or Inktomi, you search File Transfer Protocol archives (ftp) with Archie. Get it? Archie = Archives. To get to Archie sites, you need telnet.

Archie sites are quite busy, and each one is virtually identical to the other . . . they are all mirror sites. You may have trouble getting in because so many people use Archie, but there are ways around this. It is best to start out at the Archie site geographically closest to you. Listed on the next page are all the Archie sites around the world. As you know, I am living in Wyoming, so my nearest Archie site is Nebraska. What is funny is that it's also my nearest site when I'm living in California!

telnet address	location
archie.au	Australia
archie.edvz.uni-linz.ac.at	Austria
archie.univie.ac.at	Austria
archie.uqam.ca	Canada
archie.cs.mcgill.ca	Canada
archie.funet.fi	Finland
archie.univ-rennes1.fr	France
archie.th-darmstadt.de	Germany
archie.ac.il	Israel
archie.unipi.it	Italy
archie.wide.ad.jp	Japan
archie.hana.nm.kr	Korea
archie.sogang.ac.kr	Korea
archie.uninett.no	Norway
archie.rediris.es	Spain
archie.luth.se	Sweden
archie.switch.ch	Switzerland
archie.ncu.edu.tw	Taiwan
archie.doc.ic.ac.uk	United Kingdom
archie.hensa.ac.uk	United Kingdom
archie.unl.edu	USA (NE)
archie.internic.net	USA (NJ)
archie.rutgers.edu	USA (NJ)
archie.ans.net	USA (NY)
archie.sura.net	USA (MD)

If the Archie site nearest to you is busy, select one that you think might not be busy. Think of the time zone you are in, then think of an Archie site in a time zone where the majority of the people are asleep. Whatever Archie site you use, follow the steps below, or Archie will not work!

To start the search, take the following steps:

1. telnet to: archie.unl.edu

2. Login: archie

3. If you're lucky and the site is not busy, you will get a screen that welcomes you to Archie. If your local site is busy, try another site.

4. At the prompt type the key words that relate to the information that you want proceeded by the word "prog." If you are looking for fairy tales, you can use Archie to search out sites where they may be found. At the prompt "unl-archie>" type "prog fairy tales." It will look something like this:

unl-archie> prog fairy tales

If you do not know the type of command to give archie, at the prompt type help and you will receive a complete list of commands. Print these out as you will need them!

5. After pressing return, a message telling you where you are in the search queue appears on the screen as well as how long the search will take (this is not always accurate). Sometimes Archie is slow, but your patience can be rewarded with a large number of sites. Two of them are shown here.

```
                    archie.unl.edu

Host dime.cs.umass.edu     (128.119.40.244)
Last updated 08:51  4 Aug 1994

     Location: /pub/rcf/opine-dist/alpha/patches
          FILE    -rw-------    35780 bytes  09:54 18 Jul 1994  dataless-alpha-method
1
          FILE    -rw-------     4781 bytes  09:30 18 Jul 1994  dataless-alpha-method
2.gz

Host ftp.cic.net    (192.131.22.5)
Last updated 13:28  8 Sep 1994

     Location: /pub/ETEXT/pub/Politics/Feminism/Bibliographies
          FILE    -rw-rw-r--     3237 bytes  10:50 27 Jun 1994  fairy-tales.gz
```

If you can make sense out of that string of information, you are doing well. Let's try to decode the first item in the illustration on the previous page. Remember, this is first generation "stuff" that the computer savvy researchers could decode.

1. **Host ftp.cic.net (192.131.22.5)**: This says there are some fairy tales at a host or server called "ftp.cic.net" which can also be reached by its IP (Internet Protocol) number of 192.131.22.5. By the way, every Net address has an alternate IP number. You can get to any site by either form of address.

2. **Location: /pub/ETEXT/pub/Politics/Feminism/Bibliographies**: This means that you will need to go to the /pub/rcf/opine-dist/alpha/patches directory at this ftp archive to access the fairy tales file called *fairy-tales.gz*.

3. **Last updated 27 Jun 1994**: The second line tells you when the archive was last updated. It's been several years since anything has been added to the file. However, since it is a fairy tale file, being up to date is not that important.

4. Whether of not all of this information is necessary is debatable, but you did find an ftp location where fairy tales are retrievable. Now you can use your ftp software or your Web browser program and get the file you want.

ftp to: ftp.cic.net

Choose: /pub/ETEXT/pub/Politics/Feminism/Bibliographies

and find the *file fairy-tales.gz*.

Once you have decoded the returned information, quit telnet, start your ftp program, and download the files. That's the other problem with Archie — he just tells you where the files are located; he does not find them. The newer search engines on the Web are so much easier to use for that reason.

I hope you have a better idea about telnet and anonymous ftp now. They can be used to find information just like the other programs. They are helpful, but cranky, somewhat slow, and they require more computer savvy than most of us have. And that, my friends, is why gopher came about.

Gopher

Gophering is another way of working on the Internet. It's easier than telnet, and ftp, but harder than a browser. Let's jump in and try one so that all this talk will make some sense. Double-click on the icon for your gopher software (TurboGopher if you have a Mac). An advertisement appears on your screen and then a screen appears that says Home Gopher Server. My home gopher server is the University of Minnesota where the gopher program was developed. To ensure that we are all looking at the same page, pull down the file menu on your screen and click on another gopher. A dialogue box with four prompts will appear. It looks something like this:

Title:	(leave this space blank)
Server:	ericir.syr.edu
Server Port:	70 (preselected, so keep it there unless specified)
Select:	(leave this space blank)

When this dialogue box appears, type in **ericir.syr.edu** where it says "server." Note that you can leave "title" and "select" blank. The really important line is "server" for it tells your gopher program where to go. Also note that the "server port" is 70, where most gopher services live. On occasion you will be asked to type another number here. When that happens, just delete 70 and enter the new port number.

You are now at the ERIC gopher in Syracuse, New York. Here you can look at Ask ERIC files, retrieve lesson plans, and basically do all the stuff you can do at its mirror location on the Web

ERIC Web site at Syracuse
URL: http://ericir.syr.edu

The reason to access ERIC by gopher instead of by browser is simple: The Web site might be busy and the gopher location probably will not! It's another way to get to where you want to go. Also, some of the older computers (286 PCs and pre-SE/30 Macs) cannot deal with the really sophisticated browser programs, and thus gopher is all they do.

Gopher is not hard, especially after dealing with telnet and ftp! Like any of these programs, it just takes a while to dig through the maze. There are so many files, so many places to go, so many selections from which to choose, and so many different ways to get lost! When you are looking for something in particular, what do you do? You can attack the problem in one of several ways.

1. Surf until you find it (which might take forever).

2. Type the gopher address as written from some known reference point (which means you already know where you want to go).

3. Do a search with Veronica. (see below)

4. Cheat and use a search engine or directory with your web browser.

Using Your Web Browser as a Gopher

You can always use gopher the easy way by treating it like any other resource. When you are in your browser, you can access it by typing *gopher://* and then the gopher address.

Searching with Veronica

You already know how to surf, and you are probably quite good at using search engines and directories in your browser. So let's try searching with Veronica.

Just who is Veronica anyway? Depending on whom you ask, Veronica stands for "Very Easy Rodent-Oriented Net-Wide Index to Computerized Archives" or she got her name because Archie was searching ftp files, so his girlfriend Veronica

should search gopher files. Veronica, the search engine, allows you to scan gopher-space quickly for particular files and directories. By the way there is a Jughead too. He's the "find" button on Netscape, which allows you to search one document for a word or phrase.)

Here's how Veronica works. Let's use the gopher at ERIC as an example:

Select: Open Another Gopher
Server: ericir.syr.edu

At this point a screen appears that has a bunch of file folders on it, each with a different name or description. Scan down the file folders, and you will see one with a question mark (?) in it. That's Veronica's signature. If no ? is there, then read the descriptions, looking for files that say "Veronica," "Veronica Search," or "Search." (Programmers are not always consistent.) On some gophers, instead of any of the above, you will see an icon that looks like a pair of binoculars — that, too, is Veronica.

Double click on the ? (or whatever symbol is used) and you will get a small dialogue box that has a rectangular blank in it. In the blank type a word or short phrase. In the ERIC Gopher, I searched for "censorship" because censorship is a hot topic on the Internet right now. Give it a try, and you will find a plethora of articles about censorship, including some on Internet censorship. This search happens to have been a lot easier than some others I've done — often I strike out with Veronica because I do not know the right word(s) to use. You can use Boolean operators ("and," "or," and "not") with Veronica. However, if you are searching for a two or three word phrase and do not use Boolean operators, Veronica will assume you mean "and" between each word. Thus if you are searching for "League of Women Voters," Veronica will assume you mean "League and of and Women and Voters."

There are several good gopher locations you might want to visit; however, the number has not been growing as it was a few years ago. People are not investing their time in new gopher sites; they are developing Web sites with multimedia and frames that are far more colorful and powerful than anything the poor little gopher could do!

Gopher Address	Explanation
Server: unix5.nysed.gov	New York State Education Gopher is a place to find K-12 resources as well as a good Veronica search engine. A list of electronic books is available at this site too.
Server: cwis.usc.edu Choose: Other Gophers & Information Resources/Gophers by Subject/Gopher Jewels (you will need to dig to find this resource.)	Gopher Jewels is huge database with information on health, government, education, humanities, natural science, math, and more. It has a very powerful Veronica search capability. Read the information and help pages before you try to work with Gopher Jewels.
Server: archives.math.utk.edu	The Mathematics Archives Gopher provides teachers with access to public domain and shareware software as well as materials for teaching high-school mathematics.
Server: ralphbunche.rbs.edu	Ralph Bunche School Gopher is unusual . . . a school site with its own piece of GopherSpace. Check out the lesson plans, student work, and the science projects. You can also access this school on the Web.
Server: tiesnet.ties.k12.mn.us	Best of K-12 Internet Resources via TIES is like the title says. You can find information on news, online guides, books, and entry to other Gopher sites, and there is a Veronica to use when all else fails.
Server: chronicle.merit.edu	Chronicle of Higher Education is useful if you are in higher education. At this site you can read the news of Academe, look at the post-secondary job market, and see the list of the top ten books read on U.S. campuses.

Summary

Telnet, ftp, and gopher have their place, but I believe they are slowly becoming less important as the Web continues to become a larger, more user-friendly environment. You'll notice as you read information on telnet, ftp, and gopher that much of the material is over a year old. The sites are still working, but without maintenance, they soon lose their immediacy and their newsworthiness. The Web browsers are *now*, while telnet, ftp, and gopher are *then*.

Notes

Chapter 8

E-pals and Keypals

With electronic mail (email) you can engage in two-way communication on the Internet, where you can initiate a conversation as well as reply. Email is one of the more powerful and useful tools available on the Internet, and, depending on your mail program, is possibly the easiest service to use on the Internet.

When you're communicating with your keypals around the world, snail mail — a somewhat derogatory term for the postal system — becomes outdated. No more phone tag, voice mail, missed calls, lost mail, insufficient postage, or expensive overnight FedExes. (Now we have downtime, off-line links, system bugs, and the constant threat of upgrades instead!) With email, you are in direct, immediate, and almost instantaneous contact with people all around the world. (Some email transactions take overnight for delivery, depending on the technology involved; and even people who use email still forget to read and answer their mail!) With email, you can always find your correspondents, and they can always find you. In close contact, you can write messages to each other, read messages, file them, print them out for documentary evidence, and/or respond. And you can do all this without having to think on your feet in real time on the telephone. You can take your time as you ponder your replies, correct them, or even change your mind and delete them rather than send them. Then, once you send your messages, many email systems will automatically file away a copy of your reply for future reference. It's that simple and that wonderful!

Once you get an Internet account, you will automatically have an email address. To send and receive email, you will need an email software program, but so many of these are on the market, and easy to install and use, that I will not bother to attempt to list their names, discuss their merits, or explain how they work. They're all pretty much alike, except that the specific command language differs from program to program. For example, "write a message" in some programs is called "new message." And so on and so forth — you have to spend some time getting used to the quirks of whatever program you choose.

Most programs have more or less the same heading at the top of each message: a "To:" line (email address of the recipient), a "Subject:" line (space for a topic heading), a "Copy:" line (if you want to send a copy of the message to someone else simultaneously), and a "From:" line (your email address to which your correspondent may reply); some programs are more complicated than this — but not many.

Another item of similarity for all the programs is your unique address, yours alone, much like a social security number. Email addresses, while they might look long and confusing, are relatively easy to decode: Think of an email address as analogous to a snail mail address. In snail mail, you have a name, a street address, a city, a state, and a zip code. Likewise with email, you have a name (though sometimes made up of numbers and random letters), the @ sign, the server ID (equals the street address), a dot (.), location of the server (equals city and state), a dot (.), and a domain (is the zip code).

My email address, for example, is ecotton@oavax.csuchico.edu. In this case, ecotton stands for Eileen Cotton; my server is at (@) a computer called oavax, located at California State University, Chico, (.csuchico), so it is an educational domain (.edu). Quite often, the name section is the first initial and last name of the person at that address (as in my case), but this is not always the case. I have an "efriend" who has a series of numbers in the name section of her address; while this makes her anonymous, it is difficult to remember. Fortunately, many email

programs give you the ability to create nicknames so you don't need to remember long handles or difficult email addresses.

Domains other than education (.edu) will sometimes be reflected in the last part of email messages that you will receive from around the world: **.com** (commercial), **.org** (noncommercial organization), **.k12** (school district), **.mil** (military), **.net** (network), and **.gov** (government). Email addresses outside of the U.S.A. have a country abbreviation, a two-letter suffix after the domain: **.jp** for Japan, **.ca** for Canada, **.uk** for the United Kingdom, **.nl** for the Netherlands, for example. Most email addresses in the U.S.A. do not end in **.us**, but they could.

A fun exercise for your students is to collect domains or countries like some people collect stamps. See how many different countries are represented by the email they receive, then mark these countries on a world map. It's a painless way to learn geography.

Notice that I have written all the email addresses in this book in lowercase letters: ecotton, not ECotton. This is not required in this instance and certainly not by every system, but it is required by some systems. These uncooperative systems are said to be "case sensitive." It's a good idea, therefore, to get into the habit of typing all your Internet addresses in small letters, rather than large, to avoid the headache of that nasty, machine-generated reply: "Undeliverable Message."

The Power of Email

What purposes does being on email serve? You can talk with someone else about common interests. You can share news, voice opinions, compare and contrast facts and figures. It's a great way to encourage your students to read and write in an "authentic" (real-life) situation. It's electrifying to kids to realize that they are in contact with somebody in Russia, Africa, or Asia. Email is fun, easy, informative, and inherently educative, for as they say, "Travel is broadening." Now that we have email, our telephone and mail habits will change, and these changes will last our lifetime (or until the next big technological revolution happens and we're all talking on wrist-size digital color videophones!). To get your students ready for email is to prepare them for their immediate and future personal, academic, and business communications.

To communicate with someone else on email, you need the other person's address. At present, the best way to find someone's email address is to call them up and ask for it! Short of a phone call, you can try the Web and your browser at a Web site called:

Finding Email Addresses
URL: http://darkwing.uoregon.edu/~rhaller/emailad.html

Type in all or some of the information requested at a prompt box, and this search engine will try to find the email address you are requesting. Also try these sites:

WhoWhere
URL: http://www.whowhere.com/

GNN Select Internet Directories
URL: http://gnn.com/gnn/wic/wics/
internet.wp.html

Another way to find a specific address is to send an "equery" to the "postmaster" or the "Webmaster" at the site where you think the person's email account resides. People almost always include their eaddress as part of the information on their home pages. If you forget my email address, but remember my name, then either send a query to postmaster@oavax.csuchico.edu and ask for Eileen Cotton's address or look me up on our CSU, Chico home page. Most postmasters and Webmasters are very helpful.

Email Discussion Lists

At first, you and your students may have the problem of no one to send email to. A quick and easy way to solve this problem is to subscribe to a mailing list (often called a listserv or discussion list) — a special-interest group about something you are interested in. Right after you email your subscription to the listserv — probably that very day, and sometimes within minutes — you'll have more email than you have time to read (fortunately, you can always delete

messages that aren't of interest to you). After you have "lurked" on the sidelines for a while, learning the protocols of the list and the habits of the people who frequently post messages, you can take part by sending a message to the list. Your first message could be a simple one of self-introduction: "I'm new to this list. I'm interested in . . ." Someone will answer! You may be surprised at how many replies you will receive to your message. Here is where you should teach your students to be reasonably cautiousness: Just as we tell kids not to take candy from strangers and not to get in cars with people they don't know, tell your kids not to give out their phone numbers, home addresses, or credit card numbers over the Internet without permission from you or a parent.

Finding Email Lists

How do you find lists that interest you and your students? How do you subscribe? You can subscribe to lists that deal with kids, learning, education, computers, libraries, art, music, endangered species, media, sports, any content area you teach, and any subject you want. There are, literally, thousands of lists to choose from.

To receive an up-to-date list of listservs on just about any topic, send an email message to "listserv@cunyvm.cuny.edu" ("cuny.edu" stands for City University of New York). They will do a free global search about your topic and return to you a list of names and addresses of egroups you might be interested in joining. Here's how to do it:

```
To:      listserv@cunyvm.cuny.edu
Subject: (leave blank)
Message: List global/category that you are interested in
```

This search will automatically generate a list of active mailing lists matching the key word or key phrase that you type in following the forward slash (/) — where I have typed "category that you are interested in" — and then that list will be returned to you via email. When I, for example, sent the command **List global/education**, in a few minutes I received a message about ten pages long listing all the mailing lists in education — a list 10 pages long for education alone! If you prefer not to receive so much information, narrow your keyword search. A narrower search would be "education-K-12" or "education-special" or "education-arts" or whatever else you are interested in.

You can also receive similar information by using a browser on the Web. Try one of these sites:

Publicly Accessible Mailing Lists by Subject
    URL: http://www.neosoft.com/ internet/paml/bysubj.html

GNN Select Internet Services
    URL: http://gnn.com/gnn/wic/wics /internet.wp.html

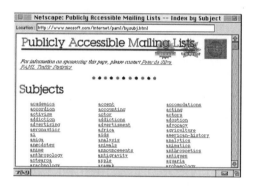

Email Etiquette or Netiquette

Before your kids start joining lists, you have the perfect opportunity to give a lesson on email etiquette or "netiquette" as it is called. Just like you have to learn which fork to use when dining, there is a protocol to learn with email. It is impolite to write a message using UPPER CASE letters, as that means you are SHOUTING at your correspondent. Don't use any four-letter words. Don't be too antagonistic when you write a message; in other words, don't "flame" (that's the lingo). The Netiquette Home Page by Arlene Rinaldi does a good job of explaining the proper rules of email and the Internet. She claims she is not the Miss Manners of the Internet, but you could fool me.

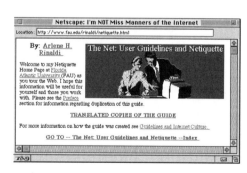

Netiquette Home Page by Arleen Rinaldi
    URL: http://www.fau.edu/rinaldi/ netiquette.html

Teachers and kids in the Net together

Because K-12 is what we do, K-12 discussion lists are a good starting point. If you don't want to look up your own lists, then you can subscribe to any of these K-12 listservs listed below:

Kidsphere Network is an excellent list for teachers, with two components: one for teachers and one for kids.

```
To:       kidsphererequest@vms.cis.pitt.edu
Subject:  (leave blank)
Message:  subscribe kidsphere <Your Name>
```

World Wide Web in Education is a large general mailing list that deals with setting up Web sites and home pages.

```
To:       listserv@k12.cnidr.org
Subject:  (leave blank)
Message:  subscribe wwwedu <Your Name>
```

ECE Net-L is dedicated to early childhood education, ages 0-8.

```
To:       listserv@postoffice.cso.uiuc.edu
Subject:  (leave blank)
Message:  subscribe ECE Net-L <Your Name>
```

MiddleL is the list for teachers, administrators, and parents who seek solutions, projects, and resources for middle schools and the "kids in the middle."

```
To:       listserv@postoffice.cso.uiuc.edu
Subject:  (leave blank)
Message:  subscribe MiddleL
          <Your Name>
```

EduPage is a bi-weekly summary of recent news items on computer technology in the schools.

```
To:       listproc@elanor.oit.unc.edu
Subject:  (leave blank)
Message:  subscribe EDUPAGE <Your Name>
```

INCLASS is a moderated list sponsored by Canada's School Net Project on the use of the Internet in the classroom from a Canadian perspective.

```
To:       listproc@schoolnet.ca
Subject:  (leave blank)
Message:  subscribe INCLASS <Your Name>
```

In emailing your subscription to any of these listservs, when I say "Write Your Name in the message field," I want you to type in your own name after you write the words that come before (and a space). This is the name to which the server will send the automatically generated reply. When I subscribed to Kidsphere, it looked like this:

```
To:       kidsphererequest@vms.cis.pitt.edu
Subject:
Message:  subscribe kidsphere Eileen Cotton
```

You will notice that I broke the rule: I spelled my name with a capital E and a capital C; I'm not e.e. cummings, after all! I wanted my name spelled right on all the messages that would come my way.

To subscribe to any online mailing list, you should use the same formula: subscribe <name of list> <Your Name>. Do not type anything else! You are going to send this message to a computer, so you can leave the subject line blank. No sense confusing the poor machine with unnecessary information. Indeed, the absolute rule when communicating with a listserv, whether to subscribe or unsubscribe or ask for other services, is to use only the specific language that system requires.

After you send the message, a response will arrive stating the rules, protocols, and FAQs (frequently asked questions) of that list, among them being this most important question: "How do I get off this list?" Save this information! I didn't do that for the first two lists I subscribed to. Later, when I needed help, I did not know how to get it, and when I wanted to get off the lists, I didn't know how. Sometimes you want to take a vacation or escape from a list for a while, and the set of FAQs tells you what you need to know to control the list's access to your email account. Deleting the instructions is a terrible mistake!

All lists have three addresses: (1) the discussion address, for ordinary purposes; (2) the automatic address, for requests that will generate automatic machine-generated administrative responses; and (3) the address of the list moderator/owner/SysOp (systems operator). If you want to discuss things on the list, use the discussion address. If you want to unsubscribe, get an archive of previous listings, find out who else is a member of the list, or get a digest version of today's correspondence, use the administrative address. If you want to talk privately to the moderator, use the third address. Try not to get these addresses confused. It is usually easier to remember the discussion address than it is to remember the other two. This is one of the few times when pencil and paper can still be helpful.

Use the moderator's personal address, not the listserv address, when you want to complain about some list member's bad netiquette or when you are hopelessly confused and don't know what to do next. The moderators of some lists look at the incoming mail and screen it for pertinence; other lists are unmoderated. For school purposes, I prefer moderated lists. A savvy, fair-minded moderator can keep a list civilized.

Lists for Kids

Lists just for kids abound. There are a number of lists to which kids may subscribe and where they will find many willing pen pals — or, rather, keypals. To subscribe to these lists, you and your students will send subscription messages that follow the guidelines stated above. Notice that the name of the list and the address to which you send your subscription are not always the same. In your subscribe command, use the name of the list, not the address.

Kids Mailing List is an international list for kids who want to send and receive messages from other kids.

```
To:       joinkids@vms.cis.pitt.edu
Message:  subscribe joinkids <Your Name>
```

Kidcafe is for 10-to-15-year-olds who want to chat.

```
To:       listserv@listserv.nodak.edu
Message:  subscribe kidcafe <Your Name>
```

Penpal-L is a list that does what its name says it does.

```
To:       listserv@uncc.edu
Message:  subscribe Penpal-L <Your Name>
```

International Email Classroom Connections is a list for teachers who are seeking classes to partner with their classes for international and cross-cultural email exchange.

```
To:       iecc-request@stolaf.edu
Message:  subscribe IECC <Your Name>
```

Other than setting up keypals, what else can you do with email? Lots! And a kid of any age who can hunt and peck out words on a keyboard can take part. Even little kids who can't write or type can dictate messages to big kids who can. The idea of having email waiting is very enticing, and most kids get excited at the discovery that there are people out there who want to speak with them.

The ease with which one generates, corrects, and deletes text on an electronic keyboard; the relative interpersonal immediacy of email; and all the many other fascinating aspects of this new toy, the computer on the Internet, make it the greatest incentive ever to early literacy. For little hands struggling to gain small-muscle control, it used to be hard to learn to write; now it's easy — and they're never too young to start.

One spring semester, I was in communication with a first-grade class, and the youngsters clearly understood what they were doing. Never think that your students are either too young or too sophisticated to participate, and don't be surprised or offended when your young students take more readily to computers and the Internet than you do. It's called the Generation Gap, and this time, you and I are on the wrong side! Turn them loose, let them go, and learn from them all you can!

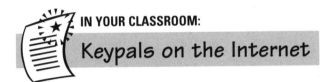

IN YOUR CLASSROOM:

Keypals on the Internet

Goal

To broaden the horizons of your students while encouraging reading and writing skills, higher-level thinking skills, and civilized discourse with other members of the world community.

Rationale

It's always nice to have someone else to talk to, to bounce ideas off of, and have a gossip fest with. It's also good to have friends all over the world in case you ever go on a long trip.

Objective

Students write and respond once a week to a keypal who is not living in their hometown. Purpose of the email correspondence is to discuss, compare, contrast, and analyze topics that are being studied in class (from weather-watching to bird-watching, work and hobbies, culture and dating habits, moms and dads, food and algebra, world events and local disasters, etc.). You must decide beforehand the exact objective you want to emphasize and you should have a class of email recipients arranged that is also working on the same objective.

Procedure

- Before starting this assignment, do the background search and identify a classroom of keypals for your students.

- Set the stage with your students by sharing some email from a list on which someone from far away talks about a topic of interest to your class or, perhaps, asks you a question about your students.

- Let your students choose from the keypals you have found to whom they want to write.

- Make sure that everyone knows how to subscribe to a list.

- Make sure that everyone finds a keypal, and that everyone gets a communication line started.

- As the semester progresses, prompt your students to engage their keypals in discussion of various aspects of topics and subjects being studied in your class.

Evaluation

By the end of the semester, your students will have gained a better understanding of, and broader perspectives on, the topics and subjects covered in your class because they will have absorbed the perspectives of their keypals. They will have experienced reading the authentic writing of other people. They will have written their own ideas in cogent and meaningful ways. They may even develop friendships that span miles.

Once your students have keypals, you and they can study geography by pinpointing the locations of email correspondents. Suggest that your class make a "country collection" (and a "domain collection," too) by looking at the suffixes at the end of each email address. You can study language arts by looking at speech patterns, letter composition, spelling, and effective ways to convey an idea to other people. Your students are accustomed to having you correct their writing in terms of its content, cogency, organization, grammar, syntax, and spelling. Ask them, now, to pass judgment on the writing of their keypals — not that your students will necessarily remark to their keypals on their English usage. If your class partners with a class of kids

overseas learning to speak English, however, your students can have great fun — and learn more language skills than ever before by being ESL teachers and teaching the other kids better American English. Your kids, in turn, might start learning another language.

You and your class can engage in cross-cultural communication, explore other points of view, learn about distant countries, and expand your knowledge of other cultures. Your kids will be fascinated to find out the similarities and differences of other children's lives.

I was scanning some keypal messages from Germany in which the students were talking about living in "terraced houses." A good question for a keypal to ask is what the difference is between terraced houses and ordinary houses.

Communicate with a class in the eastern hemisphere to find out about time zones. Communicate with a class in the southern hemisphere and discover differences in the seasons, weather patterns, and the Coriolis effect (in the northern hemisphere, water swirls down drains in the opposite direction than it does in the southern hemisphere). For older students, lists in many specialized areas are not necessarily dedicated to students, but you can screen to find adults who are willing to correspond with thoughtful kids.

The number and styles of email lessons are limited only by your students' imaginations. Use email and list participation at all grade levels. Let your lesson-planning creative juices flow, and you and your students will discover that your own classroom is the center of the universe.

Notes

Chapter 9

A Whale of a Time

Whales fascinate kids. Willy is a whale. Flipper is a dolphin.
Other deep-sea creatures from Moby Dick to Nessie to Monstro
swim through their imaginations.

Sea critters are seldom seen by us landlubbers. Think of the trouble
Captain Ahab had getting a closer look at his whale! "Free Willy" is a
movie about our bad collective conscience over keeping these magnificent
creatures — who talk and sing to one another with a greater vocal range
than humans have — in prison to satisfy our zoological curiosity. A kid
who lives on either the Pacific or the Atlantic coast may once in a while
get to see a whale or a sea lion in its natural habitat. But marine mammals
can be visited mostly in zoos and aquariums, or — like the dinosaurs —
their bones and stuffed carcasses can be viewed in museums.

Just as there are many dinosaurs lurking on the Internet, you can
also spy whales, dolphins, seals, sea lions, elephant seals, sea
otters, polar bears, walruses, manatees, and other marine
mammals. This chapter features
a Web browser-only
lesson that helps
students refine their
Internet techniques
while simultaneously
learning about some nifty
seagoing critters.

"Both at the same time" — this learning theory underlies my whole approach in this book. I offer you a painless way to teach both content and method, both subject matter and Internet savvy, and both skills and fascination. Learn how to surf the Internet masterfully and all about the sea critters — both with a few deft strokes.

IN YOUR CLASSROOM:

Sea Zoo

Goal

To develop a better understanding of the characteristics, habitats, and aquatic adaptations of marine mammals, while using some of the capabilities of a Web browser.

Rationale

Marine mammals are among the largest animals on earth. They live in the ocean, they breathe air, and they communicate quite effectively with tweets, whistles, clicks, grunts, moans, and other sounds that reverberate through both air and water. Some of them look like fish, act like fish, swim like fish, and even smell like fish, but they are not fish.

As your students learn about the marine mammals, their habitats, and how they communicate with one another, help them learn about the human attempt to communicate with marine mammals, and the Marine Mammal Protection Act. Who would want to live in a world where there were no more sea otters to swim on their backs using their chests for a kitchen table? Who would want to live in a world where the humans had eaten all the whales? Who would want to live in a world where those mermaids and mermen, the manatees and dugongs, were extinct?

A Whale of a Time

Objectives

- Use a Web browser to gather information about marine mammals.

- Show similarities and differences among the various types of marine mammals.

- Select one particular type of marine mammal and develop a three to five minute "television program" about it (or other type of report/analysis), downloading video and audio coverage, if possible, with which to illustrate the program.

- Explain the impact of the Marine Mammal Protection Act on marine mammals and fish. Determine whether the Protection Act has been instrumental in the recovery of protected species. Have groups of students complete and share with the class a K–W–L chart (see below) on a specific marine mammal. Show the similarities and differences among the several marine mammals.

Procedures

- Set the stage by showing pictures of marine mammals to heighten your students' interest.

- Brainstorm with your students about what they already know about marine mammals using a K–W–L technique:

    K – What do I KNOW about Marine Mammals?

    W – What do I WANT about Marine Mammals?

    L – What have I LEARNED about Marine Mammals?

- During the first session, your students will fill in the first two columns. After they have surfed the Net in pursuit of all kinds of marine mammals, they will fill in the last column to show what they have learned.

- Post the chart in the classroom so that, as it fills with information, everyone can see exactly what they are learning.

- Using the big K–W–L chart as a guide, propose that your students, either individually or in groups, develop K–W–L charts for a marine mammal of their special interest. They can choose from a wide variety of fields of information, such as the following: habitat; characteristics of a particular species; characteristics of individual marine mammals; locations where various species are found; pictures of individual critters; impact of the Marine Mammal Protection Act on specific groups and habitats; various marine mammals in stories, books, and poetry; scientific articles and reports about marine mammals; communication techniques of various species; human attempts to communicate with marine mammals; hunting/harvesting; and human uses of marine mammals.

- After your students have gathered their information and developed their individual or group K–W–L charts, they can use the charts as a basis for leading a class discussion on the marine mammal(s) that they have learned more about.

- From the K–W–L charts a comparison/contrast chart can be developed to show similarities and differences among the various marine mammals.

  From all the information gathering and presentations, a class database can be amassed on marine mammals, making the collective information base readily accessible.

- Using a database program, key the charted information in various categories, where it can be easily revised, expanded, corrected, enlarged, and reformatted according to a theory, bright idea, or whim. The information base then becomes a substantial basis for filling in the third column on the big K–W–L chart: "What we LEARNED."

Evaluation

The individual and group K–W–L charts, and the presentations form one basis of assessment. Establish a grade on two main premises: method and content.

Content: How much, in what detail, what kinds of knowledge, how interesting, what personal insights, what relevance to your students' own lives, what meaning derived and transferred to other aspects of life?

Method: What extent of Web surfing? How clever a use of search engines? How thorough a search? How many mirrored sites? What unexpected sites? What use of non-Web-based technology? What discovery was made through personal contact via email, lists, or newsgroups?

Use the big K–W–L chart as a class equalizer — having made sure that everyone took part in contributing to the big chart. Give it an A, and share that A with the whole class. Collaborative effort ought to result in greater results than merely individual effort. Make sure that it does!

A full Net

This unit on marine mammals may be the first solo Websurfing that your students have done. To help them get started, visit these Web sites:

Sea World Marine Mammals

> URL: http://www.bev.net/education/
> SeaWorld/infobook.html

You can find a list of links to most marine mammals at this site. The information is geared to kids. A few links are listed below:

Bottlenose Dolphins:

> URL: http://www.bev.net/education/SeaWorld/bottlenose_dolphin/
> bottlenose_dolphins.html

Killer Whales

    URL: http://www.bev.net/education/SeaWorld/killer_whale/
        killerwhales.html

Manatees

    URL: http://www.bev.net/education/SeaWorld/manatee/manatees.html

Walrus

    URL: http://www.bev.net/education/SeaWorld/walrus/walrus.html

Baleen Whales

    URL: http://www.bev.net/education/SeaWorld/baleen_whales/
        baleen_whales.html

More marine mammals

Marine Mammal WWW List

    URL: http://elpc54136.lboro.ac.uk/links.html

A general list of links to other marine mammal Web sites that is informative but written for older kids.

Bill Lemus' List of Links

    URL: http://www.rtis.com/nat/user/
        elsberry/marspec/ms_blem.html

Considered one of the best sources of Web information on marine mammals with over 50 Web sites, many of the links have marine mammal pictures as well as text.

Dolphins Rehabilitated by Texas Marine Mammal Stranding Network

    URL: http://www.rtis.com/nat/user/elsberry/marspec/tmmsn/
        rehab.html#xeno

Two personal-interest stories about stranded dolphins, how they were saved, rehabilitated, released, and tracked

Marine Mammal Protection Act

> URL: http://ash.lab.r1.fws.gov:80/./cargo/mmp.html
> URL: http://kingfish.ssp.nmfs.gov/tmcintyr/mmpahome.html

Careers in Marine Science

> URL: http://www.rtis.com/nat/user/elsberry/marspec/mmstrat.html
> URL: http://www.bev.net/education/SeaWorld/marinescience.html/
> mshome.html

Both Web sites offer the same information, a definition of a marine science program for budding marine biologists.

Marine Mammal Research Program

> URL: http://www.rtis.com/nat/user/elsberry/marspec/mmrp.html

This site includes a good list of objectives that could be incorporated into a unit on marine mammals. Comprehensive and sometimes complicated, it is a look at the interface between marine mammals and the fishing industry; for your more advanced students.

Charlotte, The Vermont Whale

> URL: http://www.uvm.edu/whale/whalehome.html

In 1849 the bones of a mysterious creature were found in Charlotte, Vermont. The bones were from a fossilized whale skeleton. Find information about this ancient whale at this Web site.

Resources for teachers and for students

Many ready-made lesson plans about marine mammals are downloadable from the Net for your immediate classroom use. You and your students can find them at the following URLs:

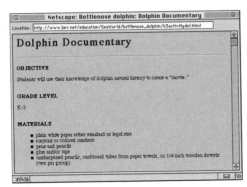

Dolphin Documentary

   URL: http://www.bev.net/education/
      SeaWorld/bottlenose_dolphin/
      k3activitydol.html

A K–3 one-day lesson plan about dolphins.

How Big Is a Blue?

   URL: http://www.bev.net/education/SeaWorld/baleen_whales/howbig.html

A one-day lesson on measuring and comparing different sizes of whales.

Orcas

   URL: http://www.bev.net/education/SeaWorld/killer_whale/
      nowhearthis de.html

A K–3 lesson on the hearing capacity of Killer Whales.

Bottlenose Dolphin: Latin Lingo

   URL: http://www.bev.net/education/SeaWorld/bottlenose_dolphin/
      48act ivitydol.html

A Grade 4-8 lesson that explains the scientific naming of dolphins. If you are working on root words and Latin derivatives, use this location.

Seals, Sea Lions and Walruses

   URL: http://www.bev.net/education/SeaWorld/Pinnipeds/introduction.html

A K-3 integrated set of lessons that weaves geography, literature, and biology of seals, sea lions, and walruses.

More Sea World Lessons

URL: http://www.bev.net/education/
SeaWorld/teacherguides.html

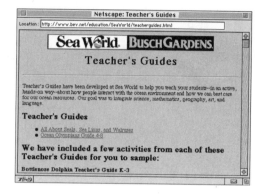

Pick your critter!

The world is a zoo, and we are but a few of the critters in it. Use the search engines, adapt the learning strategies suggested here, pick your own favorite critter and let your students pick theirs. Then, surf bravely out onto the Net to discover further information and more activities, instruction ideas and learning strategies that suit your style of teaching and your students' inclinations.

All you have to do is click on Netsearch to find home pages and whole screens full of hot links to more Web pages named birds, ornithology, domestic animals, pets, and the like. The list is so big. This must be what they meant when they said: "Learning is fun."

Notes

_____

_____

_____

_____

_____

_____

_____

Chapter 10

The News

It's hard for many kids to relate to current events. They do not yet grasp the immediate relevance of events "out there" to themselves. Their sense of interpersonal connectedness to people who they do not know personally has not yet expanded. Their process of moral development (Kohlberg, Piaget) may not have taken them even to the "us/them" stage yet.

Another cause of students' lack of connection with a world bigger than their own wants and needs is that the TV network news programs do not pitch to young people. The advertisers aim their product advertising at older folk. To kids, the news on PBS is all talking heads, slow-moving, and cerebral. The news on the commercial networks is more colorful, more active, and with more human interest, but it offers little to attract the attention of young people.

How can we make news less boring? How can make kids better informed? Can the Net help? The Internet offers action and color like a television broadcast, but — unlike TV — the Internet is not a passive medium. The Internet activates the brain rather than dulling it like TV. Hands-on Internauts don't just sit and watch; they interact. Young people's bodies, minds, eyes, and fingers move faster than old people do. If something moves too slowly, the youngsters

label it "boring." Movement on the Internet depends on who is moving. It's up to the individual users to make something.

Some students who are less interested in political and other typical news items might be more interested in sports news, which one can access through the numerous sports sources on the Net. I believe in trying almost anything to get my students hooked on the news, be it sports, up-to-the-minute reporting, human interest, disasters, or whatever. Current events are important, so I pull out all the stops to prove that they are interesting, and use the Internet to help me.

The news on the Internet comes in real time. Internauts know that you can get information from critical situations around the world faster via email, mailing lists, and Usenet newsgroups than in any other way. By reading news on the Internet, I knew more details about the Kobe earthquake 10 minutes after the first tremor than network news teams broadcasting the next morning! I also saw the newly discovered cave paintings in France before *Time* magazine published them. I can get minute-by-minute accounts of sporting events. Washington-watcher that I am, I can follow events on "the Hill" on a daily basis, read press releases from the President and speeches given by the leading political figures, and when I'm really being a glutton for punishment and politics, I can read the *Congressional Record* online. The Internet is *now*, and kids like that.

In class, you can use the Web to access the news on the Internet. You can use online personal news services either as stand-alone devices or in conjunction with the other media — newspapers, magazines, radio, television, and even short-wave radio to plug your students into the world. Here are two examples:

The Voice of America Online
> URL: http://www.farces.com/farces/
> itg-update-1.2/
> voice-of-america.html

AP Wire
> URL: http://www1.trib.com/NEWS/
> APwire.html

You can make news gathering a daily part of your curriculum. You can build a news perspective into any thematic unit that you teach. You can make learning how to find the news, read the news, and understand the news a part of your instruction in learning on the Internet.

IN YOUR CLASSROOM:

Flash! Kid reporters do the news

One way to get your students involved with the news is to have them publish their own weekly newspaper or stage their own news broadcasts. If you want them to work on reading and writing skills, set up a news publishing organization in your classroom. If you want them to work on oral communication skills, have them produce and perform news broadcasts. At the stage where they use the Internet for news-reading, news-gathering, news-understanding, and news-summarizing, the process is essentially the same, whether they will ultimately present their results through print or in person.

To set up your Internet News Bureau, brainstorm with your students what departments will be required. Local, state, national, and international news departments come to mind, as do departments for weather, sports, business, fashion, lifestyle, and human interest. You'll need an editorial department, featured columnists/commentators, a personal advice columnist, and even letters to the editor from the readers.

Let your class divide itself up into teams of Internet reporters, one team for each major department. Their tasks are to find items from the various news sources on the Internet, correlate what they find with news in print and other news media, understand and interpret what they find, and then report (i.e., write) their own news stories. (Whether they will ultimately produce a newspaper or a broadcast, they still need to write copy.)

The means of publication are up to you, your students, and the technical capabilities at your disposal. You can report the news to your class through something as simple as a weekly news presentation during which each student reports to everyone else what he or she or the team has found out.

Your class could sponsor a weekly news broadcast over the school's P.A. system. If you have closed-circuit TV in your school, you could prepare a TV news program for broadcast once a week. You could publish your class's own newspaper for distribution to school mates, parents, and neighbors. You could set up a home page on the Web, and offer yourselves, your email network, and the rest of the world your class's weekly online news digest. The possibilities are endless.

Goals

- To gain a better understanding of current events, their local and global impact.

- To get an idea of how the news is gathered and prepared for release to the public.

- To learn what it takes to produce a weekly newspaper or a weekly news broadcast.

- To learn personal, intellectual responsibility in communicating matters of import to other fellow human beings.

Rationale

Young people need to know that they are not isolated but part of a larger sphere of interest and influence that encompasses the world. By expanding their horizons, so that they think about how local, state, national, and international events all work together to "make the world go around," your students will become more active members of their global community.

Objectives

- Read news from the Internet in at least the following departments: local, state, national, international, politics, sports, business, fashion, lifestyle, human interest, weather.

- Select the best items in each department to digest and re-report in some other news media, whether a class/school newspaper or broadcast.

- As reporters, write the news, articles, editorials, etc., in each department.

- Publish the news electronically on your own home page.

Procedures

- Whet your students' appetites for news by asking them what some of the events of the last week were that really caught their attention or sparked their imagination. Discuss those items and then list them on the board or overhead transparency so that they look like the headlines of a newspaper.

- Tell your students that for the next few weeks they are going to be daily reporters, working either to publish a weekly newspaper or present a broadcast. They will be reporting the main events of the week in each of the categories listed and offering their editorial opinion on the news.

- Explore the various news resources available to them — newspapers, news magazines, radio, television, and the Internet. Don't forget their own personal reporting of the local news. Divide your class into the several news departments.

Evaluation

The students' newspaper or broadcast is the tangible result of this learning process. Did the students learn about current events. Can they carry on interesting and informed conversations about current events. What did they learn about the tricky and much-debated issues of reporters' objectivity and subjectivity. Were they able to determine whether something was newsworthy? Did their views of freedom of press and self-expression change? How?

There are too many major newspapers, news magazines, and radio and television sources to list here. Everyone has access to TVs, radios, newspapers, and magazines.

It's up to you to decide how your class will present the news. If you decide to publish a newspaper or broadcast the news, take advantage of the number of good books, teacher's guides, and periodical literature on journalism and broadcasting.

If your class decides to post its news digests on the Internet from its home page, please enter my subscription to your news service: ecotton@oavax.csuchico.edu Thanx!

Internet News Resources

This summer, there are over 1,300 newspapers on the Web. Listed below are few of the many sources of news that are readily available.

Newspaper Links

A2Z News and Information: Daily News

URL: http://a2z.lycos.com/News_and_Information/Daily_News/

This directory links to about 500 newspapers on the Web.

The University of Florida, College of Journalism and Communications

URL: http://www.jou.ufl.edu/
commres/webjou.htm

With links to commercial newspapers with Web editions all over the world, this list is rich and extensive.

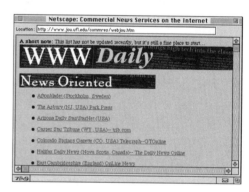

U.S. news on the Internet

CNN

URL: http://www.cnn.com/

This Web site will take you to the CNN Newspaper.

CNN TV newsroom

URL: http://www.nmis.org/NewsInteractive/CNN/Newsroom/contents.html

This URL will take you straight to the TV news room. By surfing around either of these two CNN Web sites, you will find daily newscasts with daily lesson plans, quiz items, and thought-provoking questions, all set up for teachers and students.

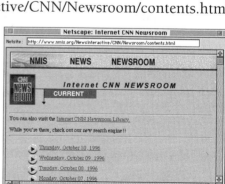

The Daily News Current

URL: http://www.newscurrent.com/

A compilation of headlines from several leading U.S. newspapers make up this Web site. It's a good summary of the news that gets updated once a day at 9:00 a.m. Pacific Time.

Nando Times

URL: http://www2.nando.net/nt/?low

This site has links to Global News, Stateside News, Sports, Politics, Business, Information Technology, Health and Science, Entertainment, Jobs/Classified Ads, and Editorials.

CRAYON

URL: http://crayon.net/

Although it does not sound like a newspaper, it is. CRAYON is an acronym (of sorts) that stands for CReAte Your Own Newspaper. CRAYON offers super-cool methods of styling your own headlines as well as links in the following categories: U.S.

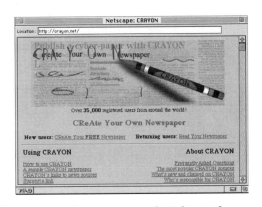

News, Regional and Local News, World News, Politics as Usual, Editorials and Opinions, Weather Conditions and Forecasts, Business Reports, Information and Technology Report, Arts and Entertainment, Sports Day, The Funny Pages, and New and Cool Web Sites. CRAYON is an excellent site to learn about how to make a newspaper work. It's a "must see" for your students, and a good jumping-off place to find out more information for each of the departments that might be included in your own newspaper.

San Francisco Chronicle and San Francisco Examiner

URL: http://www.sfgate.com/

The New York Times

URL: http://nytimesfax.com/

USA Today

URL: http://www.usatoday.com/

The Washington Post

URL: http://www.washingtonpost.com/

American politics and more

Thomas (named for Thomas Jefferson)

URL: http://thomas.loc.gov/

This Web site has links to the House, the Senate, the Congressional Record, the Library of Congress, and many other departments that focus on politics and American life. You can really keep your kids up-to-date on our legislative branch of government from here.

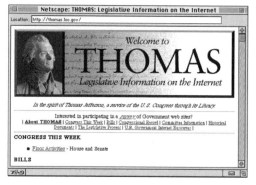

Politics Now

URL: http://www.politicsnow.com/

Here's your online connection to what is happening in politics, with the elections, and with our government. Politics Now acquires its information from ABC News, The Washington Post, the National Journal, Newsweek, and the Los Angeles Times.

International news on the Net

Online Newspapers

URL: http://www.mediainfo.com:4900/ephome/npaper/nphtm/online.htm

With links to Africa, Asia, Oceania, Europe, Latin America, the Middle East, and the United States, use this site if you want to have a more international flavor to your news collection.

Current World News

URL: http://www.yahoo.com/headlines/international/

Yahoo does a summary of international headlines and stories that is regularly updated.

Countries and Cultures

URL: http://www.yahoo.com/News/
World/Countries_and_Cultures/

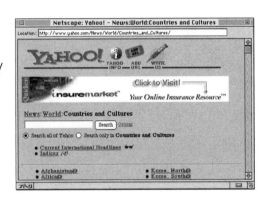

Yahoo also has links to newspapers or news agencies in 80 countries from Afghanistan to Zambia. Click on this Web site, then move to the country of interest to you.

Sports news on the Net

Sports are everywhere on the Net. Your students will find many more sites than the few I offer here.

SportsLine USA

URL: http://www.sportsline.com/

Your reporters will have a great time surfing these pages for the latest-breaking sports news.

The World Wide Web Virtual Library

URL: http://www.atm.ch.cam.ac.uk/sports/sports.html

A British Web site that features a built-in search engine, sports aficionados will never want to stop reading this book of electronic pages.

National Football League InfoWeb

URL: http://www.cs.cmu.edu/afs/cs/ user/vernon/www/nfl.html

Links to every team in the NFL can be found at this Web site.

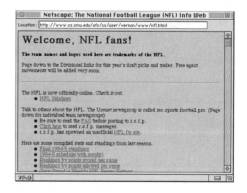

The Official Canadian Football League Home Page

URL: http://www.CFL.ca/

Links to every team in the CFL can be found at this Web site.

Baseball on the World Wide Web

URL: http://www.lmcs.edu.on.ca/ jp2/students/asmith/baseball

Maintained by Adam Smith, a high school student in Ontario, Canada, this site has links of all 28 North American baseball teams, with hot links to hockey, basketball, football, and international sports, as well.

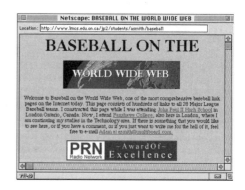

Nando Sport Server

URL: http://www2.nando.net/SportServer/

This Web site has links to football, baseball, hockey, basketball, and other sports.

National weather service forecasts

And finally, what's a news report without a wise-cracking weather person?

Yahoo Weathernewsy

 URL: http://weather.yahoo.com/

Links to weather information all around the world

USA Today Weather

 URL: http://www.usatoday.com/weather/wfront.htm

See a copy of the *USA Today* weathermap as well as forecasts for any region in the U.S.

University of Illinois, Urbana Campus

 URL: http://www.uiuc.edu/misc/weather.html

For U.S. weather maps, as well as forecasts for every state in the union, this is the Web site to visit. You will find links to the latest weather image of the U.S., current weather maps, weather movies, and a link about earthquakes.

Other news sources

I did not mention news magazines on the Web, because there are so many. However, check out *Pathfinder* at http://pathfinder.com/welcome/ which has links to *Time*, and *People* magazines, as well as links to sports, the stock market, travel, kidstuff, music, games, and more.

As you and your students work with the news, you will find many more resources and locations than I have offered here. In my experience, getting kids to become news reporters is one of the best ways for them to have fun while learning something useful.

Notes

Chapter

Look Who's Talking!

The Internet is all about communication. Nobody owns it; nobody controls it. The Internet is people conversing with one another. It's people using navigation programs and searching devices to find information. It is an international, cross-cultural society, based on the electronic communication of millions of people around the world, all talking at the same time — the greatest single conversation that has ever taken place. That's what this lesson is about.

Search engines available on the Internet are numerous, and their number and power is growing. In an earlier chapter, you learned about directories and search engines. Now you can put that knowledge to work and access some of those search devices, such as InfoSeek, Alta Vista, Inktomi, WebCrawler, Lycos, Yahoo, the Internet Directory, and others.

By using the directories and search engines on the Web, you and your students can explore the Net on a focused search — a country and a language. You will explore a country by looking at its language, people, and geography. Because we are engaging in this "global conversation," your students can gain insight into how people are the same, and how we are all just a little bit different from each other, too.

IN YOUR CLASSROOM:

Communicating with the world

As you already know, every Internet lesson needs to be goal oriented. Without a goal or an outcome, the lessons will go awry. This lesson is open ended so you can finish it anyway you like, as long as you meet the two goals:

Goals

- Learn about a country by studying its language, geography, people, traditions, and customs.

- Learn to use several Internet directories and search engines.

Rationale

From body language to electronic language (email), whether Arabic or Zulu, human beings communicate with each other — an ideal topic for study on the Internet. By studying a country, its people, language, geography, and culture, students will better understand others, and should be more prepared for the 21st century. As students become knowledge seekers, they will need to know how to use many information sources, including the Internet. They need to know how to conduct targeted information searches using several media. Using directories and search engines in pursuit of knowledge about a country will give them hands-on experience that they can transfer to searches for other sources of information.

Objectives

- Students will use several directories and search engines (you determine how many) to locate information about a country, its language, people, and geography. They will also use more traditional sources of information.

- Students will communicate via email with people from their selected country. This communication will enable them to find out about customs, traditions, values, holidays, dress, school system, economy, politics, the flag, the map, and points of interest.

- They will develop a map showing neighboring countries and language to demonstrate how the "target country" is similar to yet different from its neighbors.

- Each group will collect sets of links to home pages and Web sites that relate to the country and its language.

- Each group will produce a product — a demonstration, report, or a Web site — for the purpose of sharing their new found knowledge with other class members and with the people they have been communicating with email.

Procedure

- Set the stage by sharing magazines written in a language other than English. Share articles, pictures, and ads. Talk about what seems to be going on. Identify the languages and countries represented. Invite speakers of languages other than English to bring newspapers, magazines, and/or books to school and page through them with the class, reading, interpreting, and commenting on language and culture.

- Move to the Internet and show a few sites where the language on the screen is not English. Let you students experience the international flavor of the Internet. Keep an ongoing list of the names of various languages and their respective countries. If you want, you can put up a world map where the students locate the country of their "roots" and the language of that country.

- The Paris Pages at http://www.paris.org/parisF.html are written in French and English.

- Al-Nafitha is the first arabic magazine on the Internet. Check it out at http://www.vir.com/~smh/

- The Catalan home page in Catalan is at http://www.willamette.edu/~tjones/languages/Catalan/webcat4.html and click on http://www.willamette.edu/~tjones/languages/Catalan/webcat1.html to see it written in English.

- An English/German dictionary at http://www.tu-chemnitz.de/~fri/forms/dict.html is written in German, but you can input words in English and the German equivalent appears, or vice versa.

- A good place to start is the A2Z directory, look under language and linguistics at http://a2z.lycos.com/The_World/Languages_and_Linguistics/

- Announce the assignment. Tell your students that they will be working in small groups, using Internet directories and search engines and traditional information sources to find out everything they can about one country and its language.

- If planned ahead of time, they can communicate via email with a keypal in the target country. Encourage anyone in your class who knows another language to help classmates communicate.

- Provide guidelines for your students to follow. When kids — and adults too — surf the Web, there is a tendency to wander. To keep the assignment in focus, make it manageable. Give your students a clear set of directions or a rubric for them to follow. You might also consider showing them what to look for and what to avoid.

- Each group should create a bibliography that includes links to Web sites and other print sources, demonstrating their knowledge about a country, its language and people.

- Using the Internet is *new*, so lots of modeling is needed if you want your lesson to be successful. Consider information about the language (how many people speak it, written samples of the language, taped samples of the language, the language group [indo-European?], similar words in English), and information about the country (geographic location, type of government, political leaders, flag, customs, traditions, national dress, holidays, places of interest, schooling).

Evaluation

Have student groups share their "end product" that includes a set of links with the other groups in the class. Let other groups do short test searches, using the offered sets of links. If other students can use a set of search results to find the same Web sites and information, they've accomplished their goal.

To get them started, give your students specific instructions on how to use the various directories and search engines on the Internet. I found that the easiest way to start is using a search engine like

WebCrawler

URL: http://webcrawler.com/

With a search engine they can do a Boolean search for a country and a language, thus narrowing down the number of hits to something that might be manageable.

Set WebCrawler up so it gives you the first 25 hits and shows a summary of each hit. This way you won't be overwhelmed with too much information. By looking at the summary of each hit, you can determine if that hit will be useful to your search. You will have to model logic at this point. Teach your kids which hits look like the best one using logical deduction skills. I admit that this is far easier said than done.

After going through some of the WebCrawler hits, you might want to use a directory like

Yahoo

URL: http://www.yahoo.com/

In Yahoo, look under countries and see what evolves. Site summaries will appear when you have delved through a couple of layers of subcategories.

If your kids practice patience, you might want to consider a search in GopherSpace using Veronica. Veronica search engines are usually designated by a ? or binoculars or the title "Veronica Search" (See Chapter 7). Veronica is a search engine that uses key words. Follow the same process you did with WebCrawler. The difference between "Veronica" and a search engine on a browser is how the information is returned to you. Veronica gives information back in alphabetical order and it is not rated. You still have to choose the relevant information from the "garbage." Remind your students about bookmarks and note taking.

Each directory and search engine will produce a slightly different set of information, but as more information is gathered, similar links will appear over and over. The search for information is completed when you keep running into the same links on the Internet. Every time you see a link that is useful, save it with a bookmark. No bookmarks, no report!

The beauty of this lesson is that it allows groups to work on several things at once. You can have one or two groups working on the Internet, others using encyclopedias, atlases, magazines, or dictionaries. Allow groups of students regular periods to search the Internet. It's next to impossible to spend only 10 minutes online. (Have you ever spent just 10 minutes on the Web?)

Depending on how long you want to spend on this lesson, the information from all sources should be collected in about five to seven school days. After the students have completed the searches, they will need time to develop the information to meet your requirements.

Some good starting points on the Web

To help your students find information quicker, offer them some of the following Web sites. True, you want them to learn how to search the Internet, but sometimes the wheel has already been invented. In those cases, let your students make use of the "wheel."

The Human Languages Page

URL: http://www.willamette.edu/~tjones/Language-Page.html

This site can provide you with information about almost every language in the world. Go to the bottom of the page, and click on *Search*. In the query box, type the language you are studying, and sources will be presented to you.

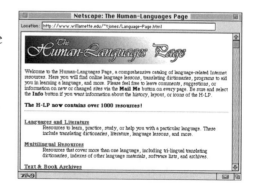

The 1995 CIA Factbook

  URL: http://www.odci.gov/cia/publications/95fact/

It has information for over 150
countries. Click on the letter of your
country, then read all the information
that the CIA has to offer. You will find
information about geography, climate,
government, economy, people,
language, education, and much more.

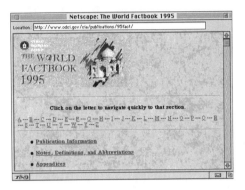

World Flags Home Page

  URL: http://www.adfa.oz.au/CS/flg/index.html

This site has a collection of flags from countries around the world. You can
also get information from the World Fact Book at this URL.

Flags of the World

  URL: http://155.187.10.12:80/flags/nation-flags.html

Here you can find pictures of flags from about 200 countries.

Planet Earth Home Page

  URL: http://www.nosc.mil/
      planet_earth/info.html

Planet Earth has information about
many countries and is easy to access.

*Links to the World at the
University of Texas at Austin*

  URL: http://www.utexas.edu/world/

Click on Cities, States, and Countries to find information about your
particular country.

Yahoo maps

> URL: http://www.yahoo.com/Science/Geography/Navigation/Maps/
> Regional/Countries/

Yahoo has links to maps around the world. It will lead you to regional maps for many countries around the world. (These maps can be copied, but they are large files and take time to download.)

Country Maps of Europe

> URL: http://www.tue.nl/europe/

Country Maps of Europe offers maps as well as some history of 46 European countries.

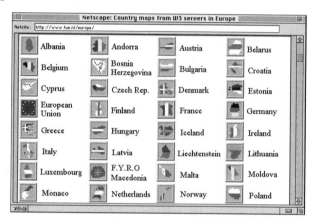

Xerox PARC map viewer

> URL: http://pubweb.parc.xerox.com/map

This site will make an HTML document of the map you want. Read the directions first, however, because this site is a wee bit complicated.

*Intercultural Email
Classroom Connections*

> URL: http://www.stolaf.edu/
> network/iecc/

This site is the link to finding keypals from around the world.

Adelante a Mexico!

I've chosen Mexico as my country and Spanish as my language on which to build my model lesson. If you use this lesson, plan your model lesson well, because your students will make many references to it while working on their country and language reports.

Before doing anything else, I checked:

The World Fact Book for 1995

URL: http://www.odci.gov/cia/publications/95fact/index.html

I clicked on Mexico. This is a good starting place for just about any country. Next, I used WebCrawler

URL: http://webcrawler.com/

I did a Boolean search for Mexico and Spanish. WebCrawler found 1,350 documents and returned the first 25, which I've listed below:

el cUCHitril: AntiVirus, Internet, Toons, Computers, . . .
Research Faculty and Staff
Chris' Specialty Meats
wingspread: chronology of textiles and fiber art
Cuernavaca Spanish Institute
The Ancient Maya Civilization
Mexico Schools
Hispanic Media Group
AMIGO! Publications Directory
Communication Connections
Univ of Toledo Spanish Bookmarks
The American Southwest—Annotated Bibliography
Mexican Genre Fiction
Things Latino-CyberRaza from EgoWeb-Ain't I beautiful?
History of Mazatlan
Tourism
Institute of Modern Spanish-Study Abroad Programs in . . .
The Spanish Beatles Page GuestBook
Welcome to Mexico!
UNAM Universidad Nacional Autonoma de Mexico 5048
el cUCHitril: AntiVirus, Internet, Toons, Comics, Compute . . .
CMI Centro Mexicana Internationl 5033
ftp://ftp.halcyon.com/pub/FWDP/International/untrtstd.txt
Study Spanish in Mexico with IUSI
ftp://ftp.halcyon.com/pub/FWDP/International/untrtstd.txt

They did not look promising at first, but I scanned down the list and saw "Welcome to Mexico!" I liked the sound of it. I scrolled back up the page and clicked on the "show summaries" prompt, and read the summary for that link.

Welcome to Mexico!

Read the newsgroup soc.culture.mexican and the Frequently Asked Questions in soc.culture.mexican, Culture and Society of Mexico, a well-organized site containing information about the newsgroup soc.culture.mexican — MexWeb. What's New with Mexico WWW. List of . . .

- Score 90% - http://www.mty.itesm.mx/MexWeb/Info2/ - Find Similar Pages

Let's analyze the "hit." Its title is "Welcome to Mexico!" The next part is a blurb or summary about the Web site, then there is a score of 90%, which means it is not a direct "hit," but it definitely has something to do with Spanish and Mexico. After that is the URL, and finally, a link for similar pages on the Web. This one looks good, so I clicked on it and saw lots of information about Mexico. Welcome to Mexico!

General Information about Mexico
- Mexico 1994 Facts from the CIA 94 World Factbook
- "Mexico's Mosaic" featuring information about Mexico
- Big Map of Mexico (U.S. CIA)
- SRE Consulado de Mexico en Nueva York

Culture and Society
- Culture and Society of Mexico, a well-organized site containing information about the newsgroup soc.culture.mexican
- Mexico Out of Balance
- Ejercito Zapatista de Liberacion Nacional
- Read the newsgroup soc.culture.mexican and the Frequently Asked Questions in soc.culture.mexican
- Mexican Constitutions (Mexico and its States) [spanish]
The Mexican Presidential Cabinet [spanish]

Today in Mexico
La Jornada
Reforma
El Norte
El Nacional

Turistic and Transportation
Subway system of Mexico City
Turistic Information on Mexico by Daniel M. German
Rec.Travel Library
Currency converter by David Koblas

WWW Servers in Mexico
MexWeb
What's New with Mexico WWW
List of ALL WWW Servers in Mexico
Sensitive Map with ALL WWW Servers in Mexico

Misc Information and Resources
Online Library Catalogs
ITESM Monterrey's General Catalog
ITESM Monterrey's Bibliographic Catalog
UDLA-P's General Catalog

Commercial Services related to Mexico

I clicked on various links and determined this Web site had to be bookmarked.
Next I opened Yahoo: http://www.yahoo.com/

I clicked on Countries under "Regional." A long list of country names
appeared, so I scrolled down to Mexico. There were a lot of links for Mexico, so
this took a while. The topics appear on the next page . . .

Cities (31)

States (311)

Indices (7)

Arts (1)	Maps (1)
Business (107)	Media (19)
Education (92)	News (9)
Entertainment (3)	Organizations (11)
Environment and Nature (4)	Outdoors (8)
Events (2)	People (1)
Government (19)	Politics (14)
Health (2)	Real Estate (13)
Internet Services (51)	Society and Culture (42)
Libraries (1)	Sports (6)
Lodging (4)	Travel (15)

My main search has two central topics: information on the country and information on the language. Given those parameters, I wanted a general set of links, so I checked the indices. There are two indices, Mexico's Index at http://www.trace-sc.com/ and the WebDirectory of Mexico at http://www.mexonline.com/websites.htm. Both of these looked promising, so I bookmarked them and searched some more.

Next, in Yahoo, I typed in Spanish in the query box and a long list of Spanish related Web sites appeared. I knew I was on the right track because there were lots of locations for learning Spanish. Here are a couple that seemed good.

Basic Spanish for the Virtual Student - fundamentals of Spanish are introduced in fifty+ brief modules: http://www.umr.edu/~amigos/Virtual/

Elementary Spanish Curriculum - prepare students to compete and cooperate in the international arena; to promote multi-cultural understanding; and to build intellectual achievement.

URL: http://www.veen.com/Veen/Leslie/Curriculum/

Another search engine to look at is:

The Planet Earth Home Page

URL: http://www.nosc.mil/planet_earth/info.html

On the query line, type Mexico
and hit return. The second item on the
list is on the Country of Mexico at:
http://www.nosc.mil/planet_earth/countries/
Mexico.html?Mexico#first_hit.

I got the following results . . .

PLANET EARTH HOME PAGE
NORTH AMERICA
COUNTRY OF MEXICO
18 DECEMBER 1995
NATIONAL FLAG
CONTENTS - Twelve Links To Get You Started
01. Mexico - The World Factbook
02. Mexico - Map With WWW Servers in Mexico
03. Mexico - Online
04. Mexico - Welcome to Mexico
05. Mexico - AMIGO! Mexico Web Center
06. Mexico - Culture and Society
07. Mexico - City Net
08. Mexico - Yahoo
09. Mexico - GORP
10. Mexico - CUI W3 Catalog
11. Mexico - List of Sites
12. Mexico - Time

My search came to an end when I started seeing repeats. From this information,
I was able to determine the best Web sites to learn more about the country and
more about the language and people. The Internet information coupled with the
information found in traditional print resources should then be collated.

As you can tell, this challenging project will take time and energy. In the end, your students will have a greater understanding of a country, a language, and the capabilities of the directories and search engines on the Internet. Start the assignment with care and move slowly as it will take time and nurturing for your students to find what they need on the Internet.

Notes

Chapter 12

Virtually Together in D.C.

In U.S. schools, students study American government several times in the course of their education. Many schools sponsor trips to Washington, D.C., every year for selected fifth graders, eighth graders, and eleventh graders. Before your students take the actual trip to Washington, D.C., they should go on a virtual tour of the city to familiarize themselves with the landscape and attractions.

On a virtual tour, your students have the ability to walk and explore where they please, even unattended, something that would normally raise chills up the spine of a parent or educator, but a smile for the student! Giving your students the freedom to travel where they want will keep them glued to their monitors. Using the Internet in such a way will engage your students and yield promising educational results.

One of the advantages I've found by using the virtual tours on the Internet is that I can plot the course of the actual trip before we leave, judging by the students' interest. We decide on an itinerary that makes everyone happy. There is nothing in these sites that your students cannot learn from.

The Internet sources that make a virtual trip possible will also make Washington more interesting when your students actually arrive there. Your students will be educated travelers, having virtually experienced the sights, sounds, history, and resources that Washington holds. Some of the sights and information your students will be able to access include: The President's House, The Department of Defense, Congress, Fedworld, The Library of Congress, The National Zoo, and of course, all the historic monuments in and around Washington, D.C. Enjoy!

IN YOUR CLASSROOM:

A virtual tour of Washington, D.C.

The first time I visited Washington, D.C., I made a startling discovery: The White House and the Capitol are two different buildings at two different locations. What a surprise! In my child's mind, despite all those news broadcasts talking about what the President had said at "the White House," as opposed to what Congress had done "on the Hill," the two had coalesced in my mind.

With this lesson, your students get used to the layout of Washington, D.C., as well as its beautiful buildings, monuments, and other landmarks.

Goal

- To give students a better understanding of the geographic layout and historically specific composition of our nation's capital, Washington, D.C.

- To get them ready and eager to go to Washington.

Rationale

Washington, D.C., is the seat of the United States government. When students know the lay of the land and the significance of the various official edifices, they develop a better understanding of our country, our government, and our representative democracy. Beginning with this geography of government, they can move on to learn more about how American government works.

Virtually Together in D.C.

Objectives

- Internet: Take a virtual tour of the federal area of the nation's capital using your Web browser.

- Cartography: Locate Washington, D.C., on a map of the U.S.A. Show where the White House, the Capitol (where the Congress meets), and the Supreme Court are located. Determine and map the best route to the Smithsonian Institution from a starting point at National Airport in Washington,D.C. Determine 10 places that seem important to visit in Washington, D.C. Draw a personal tour map of Washington, D.C., describing the tour that the cartographer would like to take.

- Historic meaning: Take a virtual tour of points of interest in the city, including the White House, the Supreme Court, the Congress, the Smithsonian Institution, the Treasury, the Library of Congress, and other important institutions in the city. Discover the significance of the Lincoln Monument, the Washington Monument, the Jefferson Memorial, the Vietnam Memorial, and other monuments and memorials in the city. Explain the differences in each of these public edifices, what they stand for, what takes place at each site, and their meaning for America. Select three or five or more "most significant" points/monuments/buildings in the city, and talk and write about their historical significance for the nation and the individual. Design a new monument for the District of Columbia, stating its significance: "Using your map and the computer, take your friends on your virtual tour of Washington, D.C., including a visit to the monument that you designed."

Procedures

- Set the stage and tell your students that they are going on a trip to Washington, D.C. Say that this trip will be a virtual tour, but that it will prepare them for an actual tour. Give them some background about the nation's capital city. This project may take a lot of preparation time, especially if you are going to escort your students on an actual trip to the Capital.

- Take this virtual tour before you start down the path to gathering travel brochures, maps, tour guides, and the expensive proposition of making overnight reservations. From the virtual tour, you will have more knowledge of what you are going to be doing and seeing so you can use your time and money efficiently.

Evaluation

By the end of the virtual tour of Washington, D.C., your students will be familiar with the important buildings and monuments in the city. Expect your students to be able to describe the various monuments and tell their significance as well as to describe some of the exhibits at the Library of Congress and the Smithsonian. Resourceful students with an interest in gardening may even be able to tell something about the National Arboretum. Students with an eye for art will be able to describe the National Gallery. Properly challenged, other students will find their own sites of special interest.

Getting started in D.C.

National Capital Parks

URL: http://www.nps.gov/nacc/

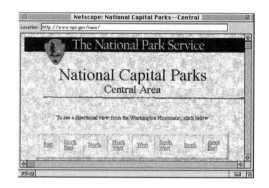

The place to go for links to the Washington Monument, Lincoln Memorial, Jefferson Memorial, Vietnam Veteran's Memorial, among other important National Park sites in Washington, D.C.

Clickable Map of Washington, D.C.

URL: http://sc94.ameslab.gov:80/TOUR/tour.html

This small (37K), and accurate, map of the federal area provides a general idea of the location of everything you are going to visit.

Travel on the Metro System in D.C.

URL: http://metro.jussieu.fr:10001/bin/select/english/usa/washington

Although it includes the location of stations and travel times between stations, you'll need a map of the city for the information at this site to make sense. (I've lived in D.C. and it does make sense, but not without additional information.)

Cheap and Safe D.C.

 URL: http://www.cais.com/npacheco/dc/dcfree.html

This slightly sarcastic visitor's guide on the Web is both tongue-in-cheek and informative. (I couldn't resist!)

The Washington, D.C. Fun and Recreation Home Page

 URL: http://www.his.com/~matson/

You can click to more than 30 links about having fun in the Nation's Capital.

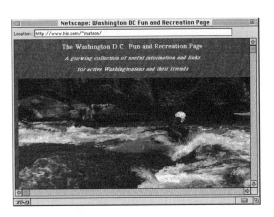

The President's House

The White House

 URL: http://www.whitehouse.gov

A trip to Washington, D.C., means a visit to the White House. At the virtual White House are links for the President and Vice President, an Interactive Citizens' Handbook, White House History and Tours, Past Presidents and First Families, Art in the President's House and Tours, The Virtual Library, The Briefing Room, and the White House for Kids. I particularly like the links for Kids and Past Presidents.

Old Executive Office Building

 URL: http://www.whitehouse.gov/WH/Tours/OEOB/

The building where the office of the Vice President is located also has historical interest as it was built for the State, War, and Navy Departments in the 1880s. See the Presidential Library and the Indian Treaty Room.

The White House Collection of American Crafts

    URL: http://www.nmaa.si.edu/whc/whcpretourintro.html

American crafts made from ceramic, wood, fiber, metal and glass are displayed at this Web site.

The Department of Defense

    URL: http://www.dtic.dla.mil/defenselink/

The Web site with links to each branch of the military, the Pentagon, as well as to daily news briefings from the Secretary of the Department.

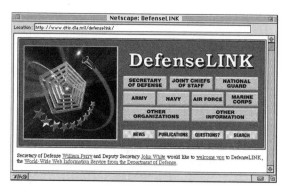

The Congress

The other unavoidable house to visit is the one with the big dome up on Capitol Hill, the United States Congress. Before planning an actual visit to Washington, D.C., email your Senators and Representatives and tell them the dates you will be in the city. Congressional staff members will respond via snail mail with tickets to the House or Senate galleries and maybe even tickets for an actual White House tour.

The House of Representatives

    URL: http://www.house.gov/

The Senate

    URL: http://www.senate.gov/

Thomas (named for Thomas Jefferson)

URL: http://thomas.loc.gov

This is the best source for everything about the Senate and House of Representatives, the Congressional Record, and important speeches from the last two congresses, as well as information on how the legislative branch of government works. I've already mentioned Thomas in

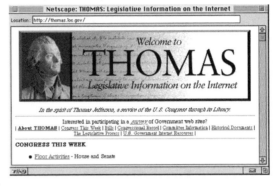

chapter 10, but it's well worth another mention in a chapter on D.C., and it's worth a bookmark, too.

CapWeb

URL: http://policy.net/capweb/congress.html

Other Sources of Government Information

URL: http://www.senate.gov/other/gov_other.html

Other branches of government

Other Departments of Government

URL: http://www.law.vill.edu/Fed-Agency/fedweb.exec.html#feddept

Links to all the Cabinet level agencies in the government are at this site.

The Treasury Department

URL: http://www.ustreas.gov/
treasury/homepage.html

Find out all there is to know about the Treasury Department, and you can link to a picture of the newly redesigned $100 bill.

$100 bill

> URL: http://www.ustreas.gov/
> treasury/whatsnew/newcur/

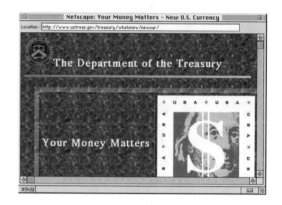

The Federal Bureau of Investigation

> URL: http://www.fbi.gov/

Among other things, find out about job opportunities with the FBI, and the 10 most wanted list.

The Department of Justice

> URL: http://www.usdoj.gov/

Talk to the Attorney General. This site is also a mirror site with links to other federal government departments, including the Departments of Agriculture, Commerce, Defense, Education, Energy, Health and Human Services, HUD, Interior, State, Transportation,

Veteran Affairs, and Education. For a set of links to almost every department of government, go directly to URL: http://www.usdoj.gov/other-link.html

FedWorld

> URL: http://www.fedworld.gov:80/

A list of links to other governmental departments including the IRS.

Library of Congress and the Smithsonian

The cultural life of Washington is rich — museums, scientific institutions, art galleries, libraries, and more. D.C. is a showplace to the world of the best that America has to offer.

Library of Congress Virtual Tour
   URL: http://www.loc.gov/

At this site you can view online exhibits.

American Special Collections
   URL: http://lcweb.loc.gov/spcoll/full.html

The Library of Congress Cultural Exhibits
   URL: http://lcweb.loc.gov/homepage/events.html

The Smithsonian Institution
   URL: http://www.si.edu/newstart.htm

Follow the links to find out information about each of the various museums that make up the Smithsonian Institution. Here are some of the sites:

The Natural History Museum
   URL: http://nmnhwww.si.edu/nmnhweb.html

Air and Space Museum
   URL: http://www.nasm.edu/

National Zoo

    URL: http://www.si.edu/organiza/museums/zoo/homepage/nzphome.htm

The Smithsonian Gem and Mineral Collection

    URL: http://galaxy.einet.net/images/gems/gems-icons.html

You and your students will find many more Internet sites on Washington than I have provided. Web surfing is fast becoming a standard activity of people engaged in serious life-long learning, so expect more sites each time you teach this lesson. To go along with what you can discover via the Internet, use other electronic  library resources that are available, such as Encarta, a CD-ROM program with a lot of great information about Washington, D.C.

What it means to me

For a culminating activity, have students, either individually or in groups, select the three or five or more (a number suitable to you and to them) "favorite places" they want to visit in Washington, D.C.

Have them design a quick virtual tour for their classmates, showing and explaining the places they want to visit, and telling why those places are significant to them and to the country. If each group in your class selects three different sites, they will have organized a thorough virtual tour of the city that will get them all ready for the actual tour.

For a thought-provoking, highly meaningful capstone on this project, propose that each student design his or her own D.C. monument, draw a sketch of it, and be ready to explain the following to the class: what it would look like; what it is; where it would be in D.C.; what does it mean?

The results of this exercise might make an interesting contribution to the Web via your class home page (see Chapter 5): "Our Class's New and Improved Washington."

Other tours

After your students have taken a virtual tour of the Capitol, they will be ready to learn more about the workings of the American government. You can develop that lesson yourself by using a search engine, with a few of the following key words: government, legislative branch, executive branch, judicial branch, senate hearings, government documents, declaration of independence, constitution, amendments.

If you and your students would like to take a virtual tour of another city, state, or country, go to:

Virtual World Tours

   URL: http://www.dreamscape.com/frankvad/world.html

To design virtual tours of other cities, you can make a tour of the city of your choice to suit yourself by using directories and search engines that are accessible from your browser. A virtual tour of your hometown can be a challenging class project and would look great on your class home page.

Notes

Chapter 13

The Games People Play

Here it is — computer games on the Internet! Just what you've been waiting for! You were probably thinking that your kids spend too much time playing video games. If they would only invest some of that time on studying, they would corner on the market of electronic knowledge.

Face it! Kids play. In fact, play is kids' work, so why not show them some good, clean, healthy electronic playgrounds on the Net! That, alas, is easier said than done. All kinds of games are available on the Internet. Unfortunately, even games that at first blush may look like they're okay for kids could eventually cause a lot of blushing. The Internet is the world, and, as the saying goes, "It takes all kinds." There are some very "adult" games on the Net.

As with video games at the mall, some of the games on the Net are barbarously violent and gory. Some are sexually explicit, while others are filled with language bad. A few sites rely on gambling skills — virtual slot machine, poker, and blackjack.

If you don't want your kids visiting these inappropriate Web sites, then you will not want to put a general games list in your bookmark collection. You will want to be more selective. Steer the kids away from the disapproved games by steering them towards the games that you do approve.

Our role, as teachers, is threefold:

1. Establish standards that you think are appropriate for your classroom.

2. Check out the Internet sites to make sure that they meet your standards.

3. Uphold your standards with your kids. Engage them in any necessary discusions that are helpful in persuading them to understand your point of view. Assist them in learning how to discriminate the appropriate from the inappropriate.

Managing Games in the Classroom

This might be time to review your Acceptable Use Policy or AUP that we talked about in Chapter 3. Remember what was agreed upon in your AUP and enforce it. In addition, some Internet servers have blocking programs. There are also numerous commerical blocking software on the market, such as CyberPatrol. In fact, the latest version of Microsoft Internet Explorer has a built-in rating system for users to control the amount of violence, sexual content, etc.

While games might not be top priority in your classroom, remember that students can learn several things by working with games. First and foremost is how to download and decompress files. Most games are large, so they have been compressed and placed at ftp sites. If your students download a game, they get practice at using ftp procedures. They also get practice at decompressing programs; checking for viruses; installing the programs on a hard drive; and then deciphering the game. This is a good set of skills to master. It can be easily transferred to other types of files and programs.

There is also the issue of "multiple intelligences." According to Howard Gardner, among the seven "frames of mind" are the logical-mathematical and the bodily-kinesthetic. Both of these intelligences love games: mind games for the

logical-mathematical, and physical games for the bodily kinesthetic. Just because something on the Web or in school is not about reading, writing, and arithmetic does not mean that it is not educational nor that it is not essential to the development of one of the frames-of-mind hard-wired in our brains. The "literate frame of mind" is neither the only, nor the most important intelligence.

Enough said. Let's go and look at what games are out there that you can use in your classroom. We'll make up a general list and then you can pick and choose for your class. It's a good idea to build you own top 10 list and store it in your bookmark collection.

Here are a few general game sites that you might want to look at.

Many Games

Games Domain

URL: http://www.gamesdomain.com/

This list has regular updates with links to games on the Web as well as games that can be downloaded. There is a list of ftp sites for freeware and shareware games for all types of computers (Macintosh, PC, Unix, Amiga, etc.). Check out the ftp sites at this site.

Two other good game sites are:

Jumbo

URL: http://www.kidscom.com/adults/

Happy Puppy

URL: http://happypuppy.com/games/

Yahooligans

URL: http://www.yahooligans.com/

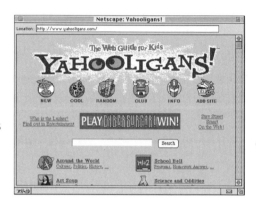

Click on Computer/Games. A list with more than 25 links will be the next thing you see on your monitor. Yahooligans is Yahoo for kids. The links have been selected, so there might be some mechanism to keep them kid-oriented. However, many of these general game sites are not for the faint of heart. There are lots of blood, guts, gore, and violence attached to some of these games.

Games Online

There are also Web sites where you can actually play games online. I personally feel that this is a use of expensive Web time. It should be completely justified. Now, after I say that, I was checking out game sites, and got completely lost in a game of Webtris, so be careful. These sites can be dangerous eaters of time. I like Tetris. It teaches spatial awareness, the knack we need for the creative cramming of stuff in drawers and small refrigerators and moving vans. When my nephew moved to a new apartment, he said that Tetris had really helped him pack the trailer because he could visualize better how the chairs looked, turned upside down and backwards. If you want to get lost in Webtris (a web version of Tetris), go to this site in the United Kingdom:

Webtris

URL: http://www.blueberry.co.uk

You will notice that this leads to "Gid's Games" where many of the games are Web interactive. That means, several people can log on to a game at the same time, and play it. You never really know if you have control of the board which makes trying to figure out strategy very difficult. Other games at this site include The Logic Board (like Mastermind), Flipper, SOL, The Cube (Rubic's Cube, that is), and one called Berries.

For a nice easy game of Tic-Tac-Toe, visit this site:

Tic-Tac-Toe

URL: http://linex.com/~donham/ttt.html

There are three modes of play: very easy, easy, and hard. You can choose to be X or O. This is an excellent game of strategy and sportsmanship, and your kids do have to think to make T-T-T work. A more difficult version of Tic-Tac-Toe is the three-dimensional variety, which you can find at

Tic-Tac-Toe 3D

URL: http://www.hepl.phys.nagoya-u.ac.jp/cgi-bin/3dttt

This address offers no directions for getting the game to start, but it's easy. Point and click, and it will go. Then wait for the computer to make a move, and then point and click again. The X's and O's will appear magically on the screen before you. The game keeps a winner's list of the names of people who have been successful at it.

Boston College has a Interactive Games site on the Web page.

Boston College Games

URL: http://www.bu.edu/Games/games.html

At this site you can play several logic games that pit you against a computer. The computer usually wins. The Peg Game, Tic-Tac-Toe, Minesweep, Hunt the Wumpus, and a 9-puzzle are non-Java games. They also have Java versions of Battleship and 9 Puzzle. The Java games are faster than the non-Java games, but you must have a browser that supports it. That means Netscape 3.xx or Internet Explorer 3.x.

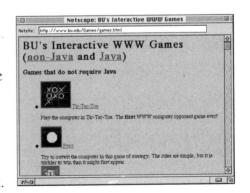

Chess, anyone?

Chess games are abundant on the Internet. I recommend that you conduct a search with the Lycos Search Engine. In the query box type "chess" and you will find a ton of Web sites. I wish I could give you more information about which site is the best, but this is one game I've never been able to get into. This is one of my many shortcomings. What can I say?

If you want to download games to your own or the class computer, heed my warnings. The sites are busy. They contain a lot of games you might not wish your students to play. When you find something offensive, don't blame me: My advice is the old saying, "Pick the roses and leave the thorns."

CyberComics

There are a number of comic book characters that have home pages. Using Yahooligans, you'll find links the following comics on the Web:

Comic Links on Yahooligans

URL: http://www.yahooligans.com/The_Scoop/Comics

- Calvin & Hobbes Jumpstation:
  The - Directory of Calvin & Hobbes Web sites.
- Comic Strip: Access Various Comics
- Far Side by Gary Larson
- Hometown Heroids - Comic strip about an out-of-work superhero.
- Incredibly Complete Tick Links Page
- Marmaduke
- Peanuts: Snoopy's Dog House
- Philadelphia Online Comics - Create your own comics page!

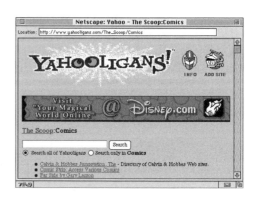

Create your own games

You can create your own games using the resources on the Net. You can develop games for your class to play based on television shows such as Jeopardy or the Wheel of Fortune. You can also design games based on popular board games such as Trivial Pursuit or Monopoly. You can also invent computer-aided games based on tried-and-true classroom games that have been used for eons.

For example, play "Web Page 20 Questions." Find a big Web site with links to lots of other pages. Luckily, these big pages are available on just about any subject area you can think of and a few are listed in other chapters of this book. Use your browser to find megapages in your subject area or field of interest. You can do an InfoSeek Search for "Bosnia" and come up with 10 home pages that might be of interest. Select one that best suits your purpose.

"Web Page 20 Questions" has two parts: First, the player has to find the right Web site, and second, the player has to answer the 20 questions by linking from the Web page to another. Here's a "Web Page 20 Questions" that I developed that you might want to use as a model.

Web Page 20 Questions: "Cats"

Step A: Find a Cat Page that shows breeds.
　　　　For instance, go to one of these sites:

Breed Pictures & Profiles
　　URL: http://www.csd.net/~abyman/breed.html

Step B: Answer these 20 questions

1. What is another name for an Angora cat?

2. What type of cat has no fur?

3. What type of cat is Socks?

4. When is a cat given the title GC?

5. Why do people like cats?

6. How old should a cat be in order to be adopted?

7. How much does it cost to subscribe to the Cat Fanciers mailing list?

8. List the common cat colors are there? List them.

9. Compare a Japanese Bobtail to a Manx.

10. How is a Colorpoint Cat different from a Siamese Cat?

11. Describe Balinese cats.

12. Draw a cat.

13. Judge the coolest cat and explain why.

14. You are a dictionary writer. Give four definitions of "cat" from serious to humorous.

15. List five properties of a Manx cat.

16. Write a poem about a pet cat.

17. Create a new reason for having a cat.

18. If your cat was pink, how would it react on a rainy day?

19. Describe how a cat might access the Internet.

20. You want to give a kitten to someone special. How would you wrap it up?

Answers to most of these questions can be found at one location with a bit of surfing. Questions 16-20 use imagination. I think you can see the value of this type of game. Kids are on a scavenger hunt looking for specific information, while skimming and scanning a complete web site. It's a very painless way to learn.

In the beginning, you can model questions devising this game for your students. Make it as easy or as hard as is advisable for the age of your students and their degree of ability at surfing the Web. Later, have the students work in teams to make up games for others to try. The teams can play against each other. Team members learn when they invent their games and again when they play their rival's created games. Teams should try and make to their game harder than the others. Keep score whichever way you think is best.

Here are some interesting big Web sites that would make great "Web Page 20 Questions" game starters:

Castles on the Web
> URL: http://fox.nstn.ca/~tmonk/castle/castle.html

Dino-Sauria OnLine
> URL: http://www.dinosauria.com/

The Maya Astronomy Page
> URL: http://www.astro.uva.nl/
> michielb/maya/astro.html

The Sun Page
> URL:
> http://www.hao.ucar.edu/public/education/
> education.html#additional.haoh_edu

Hunt and Peck

A simpler, easier computer-aided game that you can play with your students using the Internet is "Hunt and Peck." Download a short story or poem from the Net or require the game-player to download the file. Put it in a file with a number of questions about the text. The player must answer each questions. For this game, you can find short stories and other pieces on the Net at several URLs.

I've always loved the imagery in the wonderfully nonsensical poem, "Jabberwocky," by Lewis Carroll.

Jabberwocky
> URL: http://pubweb.parc.xerox.com/hypertext/whimsy/jabberwocky.html

Jabberwocky Variations Web site
> URL: http://www.pobox.com/~keithlim/jabberwocky/

I actually like the variations site a little bit better as it has translations of the poem in a zillion languages, plus parodies that are a good springboard to other lessons you can develop from the original.

Hunt and Peck: Jabberwocky on the Web

Here is a game of "Hunt and Peck" that I devised for "Jabberwocky":

A. Find "Jabberwocky," by Lewis Carroll, on the Web.

B. Download the poem and put it in the file with "these questions."

C. Answer the following questions based on "Jabberwocky,"

1. Draw a Jabberwock.

2. Create a new action word for the Jabberwock to do. Define the word and draw a picture of the Jabberwock doing it.

3. Describe slivvy? Why would you want one? Argue your case.

4. Pick out another word in the poem. Define it. Why would you not want one? Argue your case.

5. Why should you beware the bandersnatch? What will happen if you are not cautious of one?

Games and laughter

Games and jokes — allow them to have their place in your online classroom! They serve more purposes than diversion, comic relief, relaxation, or reward. Games teach us to be logical, precise, and strategic in our thinking. Because many (not all!) of your kids enjoy games, they will learn a lot as they devise their own. Games can serve to reinforce skills and knowledge that you have been teaching. Maybe that's the best part — the kids learn, have fun while they're doing it, and don't even notice that they are learning. That's winning the best game of all — the Teacher Game!

Chapter 14

The ABCs of the Internet

A is for Archie, B is for Browser, C is for Computer. . . .

Alphabet books are among the first texts that little people read. The goal of this lesson is for older kids to use the Internet to make an alphabet book for younger children.

The topic can be about anything, as long as it's broad enough to offer plenty of words to use up the alphabet. An easy ABC book would be on animals. The older students would probably start with Aardvark and end with Zebra. The challenge for them would be finding information about these critters on the Web. Once they had finished their work, arrange for a cross-grade peer collaboration between the two grades, for example, a fifth grade class with a third grade class.

Place a couple of older kids and a couple of younger ones in front of the same computer. Let the older students show the younger kids their ABC project. Then let older kids and younger kids surf the Web together in search of more animals. The fifth graders could teach the third graders how to browse, and the third graders can show off their computer skills, too.

ABC books are easy to create, because they deal with topics we already know. Now, let's focus on a topic that might be more challenging and less familiar. Let's make an Online ABC Book of Canada.

We study Canada in both middle school and high school. But U.S. study of Canada tends to be inadequate, at best. Most Canadians with a high school education know infinitely more about the United States than our students know about Canada. For example, most of us don't know that the U.S. attempted to conquer and annex Canada in 1812, but failed at the Battle of Queenstown Heights. Canadians, you may be sure, know this! And this is only the beginning of the "Yanks" ignorance about "the True North." After typically inadequate study of Canada by U.S. school kids, they still often don't know that Canada is the largest country {in terms of land mass) in the world, yet with a total population smaller than that of California. Most don't know that Canada is divided into provinces and territories. Most of us don't know that the United States and Canada share one of the longest open, unguarded borders in the world. Only the American tourist to Canada finds out that Canada has a dollar coin, nicknamed "the Loonie." If your kids do not yet know this kind of information about our magnificent northern friends and relatives, then it's time to get them cooking on the Web to find out more about Canada.

IN YOUR CLASSROOM:

The ABC Book of Canada

Goals

- To gain a better understanding of Canadians, their land, geography, and government; their culture, history, and ethnic heritage; and their thoughts and feelings about U.S. citizens.

- To begin the assembly of a body of information so that students can compare U.S. culture with another culture.

Rationale

The Land of the Maple Leaf is the United States' largest and most important trading partner. One of the two official languages of Canada is English; this means that U.S. citizens can speak their own tongue and be understood almost anywhere they go in Canada. Canada is the country to which many are most likely to travel. Part of the fun of studying Canada is finding out the ways in which they are "just like us" and the ways in which they are "different." Because Canada is part of the course of study in U.S. schools, let's use the Internet to help us do a good job of finding out about our cousins to the north. Surf the Web and take a Canadian vacation without leaving home.

Objectives

- Gather information about Canada from all kinds of sources on the Internet for comparison with knowledge about Canada gained elsewhere.

- Choose the best articles, pictures, databases, lists, newsgroups, maps, and other sources about Canada.

- Write an ABC book on Canada (at whatever level of sophistication the individual student is able to work), one that can be shared with kids from a lower grade or retained for use by a subsequent class. The ABC Book should include maps, charts, flags, pictures, and text.

Procedures

- Set the stage by reading an ABC book to your class and letting them talk about the ABC books that they had "back when they were children." Hold a discussion about the elements of an ABC book. Propose making an ABC book that can be shared with another class. Talk about Canada, activating your students' prior knowledge about Canada and proposing that Canada be the topic of the ABC book. Using the suggestions below as well as whatever your students themselves find on their own, explore the Internet for information about Canada, relating this to any other information about Canada available from any other sources.

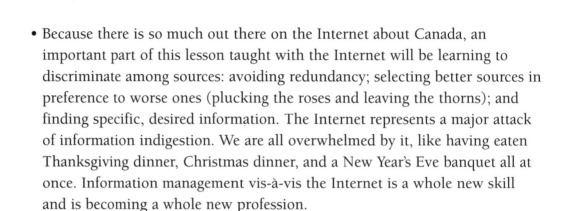

- Because there is so much out there on the Internet about Canada, an important part of this lesson taught with the Internet will be learning to discriminate among sources: avoiding redundancy; selecting better sources in preference to worse ones (plucking the roses and leaving the thorns); and finding specific, desired information. The Internet represents a major attack of information indigestion. We are all overwhelmed by it, like having eaten Thanksgiving dinner, Christmas dinner, and a New Year's Eve banquet all at once. Information management vis-à-vis the Internet is a whole new skill and is becoming a whole new profession.

- Suggest that your students use the strategies in Chapter 8 to find keypals in Canada. These direct connections with Canadian students will be an excellent way to test first-hand the archival information that your students discover on databases. Because most Canadians speak English, an email connection with Canadians is easy.

- You may want to divide your class into several groups, each group working on a different type of alphabet book. You may also want the groups to be responsible for a segment of the alphabet, such as A-E, F-J, K-O, P-T, U-Z. (Because A-E is inherently easier than U-Z, you might want to mix the letters up: Group 1 = A, F, K, P, U; Group 2 = B, G, L, Q, V;, Group 3 = C, H, M, R, W; Group 4 = D, I, N, S, Z; and Group 5 = E, J, O, T, Y, Z.)

- When the Internet work has been completed, and the ABC Book of Canada is ready for publication — whether in hard copy or online — partner your class with a class at a lower grade level so that your students may share their information about Canada with the younger kids, and, at the same time, teach them something about the Internet.

- Before the cross-grade collaboration, give your students some guidance in what to expect from the younger kids, how to relate to them, how to show them the book, how to let them enjoy the book, and how to explore the Internet with the little kids. Allow the younger ones to have their hands on the keyboard to facilitate learning.

Evaluation

Compiling the several groups' work, your class can produce its full ABC Book of Canada for sharing with another class. The process of bringing the various parts and pieces together can become a beneficial formative assessment, because each group evaluate its own and other works. Decisions will have to be made about what to include and exclude, balance, style, focus, look, feel, and the specifics of typography and book production.

You can make this book simple or complex, and it can take whatever form you choose. One major proof of the pudding will be in how well your class project goes over with the kids in the class down the hall.

Another point for students to keep in mind as they produce their book is audience. After the cross-grade collaboration, engage your students in a discussion of how it went with the little guys. Remind your students of the points you will have made in preparing them to work with the younger class, and use those suggestions, now, as a check list against which to evaluate the collaborative experience. This evaluation will be a self-assessment.

How to Visit Canada via the Internet

Yahoo: Canada

URL: http://www.yahoo.ca/

Yahoo has its own Web site in Canada. From this directory you can find information on each province and territory. This is probably the first site to visit to get an idea of the scope of information that is available about Canada.

Map of Canada

URL: http://www.lib.utexas.edu/Libs/PCL/
Map_collection/americas/Canada.GIF

Get a feel for the size of the country by looking at this color map.

Provincial and Territorial Sources of Information

> URL: http://www.droit.umontreal.ca/opengov/provinces.html

Click on the flag of a province or territory to find out more information about it (a colorful Web site in English or French).

Federal Links

> URL: http://canada.gc.ca/depts/
> major/depind_e.html

An alphabetical listing of links to every department in Canadian government.

CIA Fact Book of Canada

> URL: http://www.odci.gov/cia/
> publications/95fact/ca.html

A text-only link that tells you about the geography, economy, people, and everything else about Canada.

The Flags and Arms of Canada

> URL: http://www.cs.cmu.edu/afs/cs.cmu.edu/user/clamen/misc/
> Canadiana/CA-flags.html

Get a look at the flags and coat of arms for each province and territory

Canadiana: The Canada Resource Page

> URL: http://www.cs.cmu.edu/afs/cs.cmu.edu/
> user/clamen/misc/Canadiana/README.html

This general information page is a huge site with links to news and information, facts and figures, travel and tourism, government, politics and history, science and education, technology, heritage, culture and entertainment, and finally general links.

Defacto: Geographical Facts About Canada

> URL: http://www-nais.ccm.emr.ca/
> defacto/

This Web site reads like a trivia game.
Where is the longest river in Canada?
How many lakes are there in
Saskatchewan?

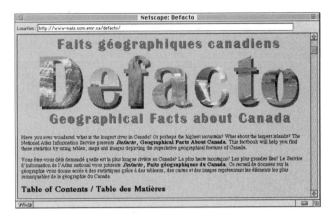

Tour of Canada Without
Leaving Your Desk

> URL: http://www.cs.cmu.edu/afs/cs.cmu.edu/user/clamen/
> misc/Canadiana/Travelogue.html

All the links you need to see, hear, and read about Canada. This is like the
virtual tour of Washington, D.C., only bigger.

Canadisk

> URL: http://schoolnet.carleton.ca/cdisk/

If you know the questions to ask, you can ask them here. A part of
Canada's Schoolnet, this Web site is designed for students of Canadian
studies. You can also go to

Schoolnet

> URL: http://schoolnet.ca

Canadian Government Information
on the Internet

> URL: http://library.uwaterloo.ca/
> discipline/Government/CanGuide/

Leads you to information about the
peoples, provinces, and territories of
Canada.

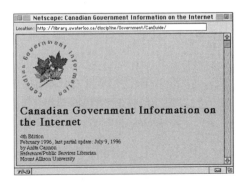

Canada Historical Documents

> URL: http://WWW.Screen.COM/CPACf/program/resources/
> English/hist.html#FED

You can see the text versions of the Canadian Charter of Rights and Freedoms, The Constitution Act of 1867, the Meech Lake Accords, as well as information about the Canadian confederation.

The Canadian Press

> URL: http://xenon.xe.com/canpress/Overview.html

Go here to see news from the Canadian perspective.

Geologic Survey of Canada

> URL: http://www.emr.ca/
> gsc/texthp.html

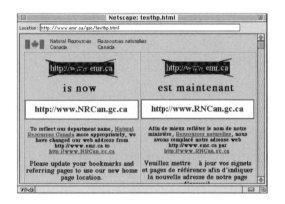

Click on Educational Materials and News to find the geologist. You can get information on subjects from earthquakes to gravity. You can also ask a geologist a question via email.

Geodetic Survey of Canada

> URL: http://www.geod.emr.ca/

This site allows you to search for information about the geography of Canada, as well as links to information about the government of Canada.

Weather from Environment Canada

> URL: http://www.doe.ca/
> weather_e.html

Here's where you can get weather forecasts for every area of Canada, as well as maps, charts, and satellite imagery. In Canada, temperatures are shown in degrees Celsius, not Fahrenheit. This would make a good exercise for converting one temperature system to the other.

Let's get started

To start your students thinking about Canada in Internet terms of the ABCs, they can surf the Canadian sites mentioned above to answer the questions below, filling out the URLs as proof of their discoveries. After they have practiced using this page, it's their turn to make up their own 26 letter ABeCeDarium of something.

An Internet ABeCeDarium of Canada

A is for Aleut — *URL: http://*_____

How many Native Canadian peoples can you name?

B is for Banff — *URL: http://* _____

Where is Lake Louise?

C is for Calgary Stampede — *URL: http://* _____

Who does the stampeding?

D is for Dogwood (provincial flower of B.C.) — *URL: http://* _____

Where is British Columbia?

E is for Elizabeth the Queen — *URL: http://* _____

Is the Queen of England still the Queen of Canada?

F is for French language — *URL: http://* _____

Where do they speak French in Canada? How many people speak French there? How many people speak Ukranian and other non-English languages?

G is for Gaspar Bay, Nova Scotia — *URL: http://* _____

How cold does it get in the northern parts of Canada?

H is for Hudson's Bay — *URL: http://* _____

What was the Hudson's Bay Company, and for whom was it named?

I is for Inuit — *URL: http://* _____

Now how many Native Canadian peoples can you name?

J is for Jasper National Park — *URL: http://* _____

Do Canadians or Americans do a better job of taking care of nature?

K is for Kingston, Ontario — *URL: http://* _____

Who named Kingston and why?

L is for Loonie — *URL: http://* _____

What's a loon?

M is for Maple Leaf Flag — *URL: http://* _____

What else in Canada is called "the Leafs?"

N is for Niagara Falls — *URL: http://* _____

Half of Niagara Falls is in Canada; where is the other half?

O is for Ottawa — *URL: http://* _____

What is the structure of Canadian government? Can you name all of the provinces and their capital cities?

P is for Parliament and the Prime Minister — *URL: http://* _____

How does Canadian government differ from American government?

Q is for Quebec City — *URL: http://* _____

Quebec City is the only walled city in North America and the capital of New France. What else is called "Quebec?" How do the Quebequois pronounce "Quebec?"

R is for Regina, Saskatchewan — *URL: http://* _____

Who was the Regina they had in mind when they named the town?

S is for Saint Lawrence Seaway — *URL: http://* _____

From where and to where and between where does it run?

U is for Union Corner Provincial Park, P.E.I. — *URL: http://* _____

What are the Maritimes?

V is for Victoria Island, B.C. — *URL: http://* _____

Where does America stop and Canada start? What is the Pig War?

W is for Winnipeg, Manitoba — *URL: http://* _____

Where do people get the strange names that they give to their cities?

X is for xenophilia — *URL: http://* _____

What is the basic Canadian attitude toward foreigners?

Y is for Yukon Territory — *URL: http://* _____

Gold fever! What can you find out about the American gold rush
into Canada?

Z is for Zones — *URL: http://* _____

How many time zones does Canada have, and how do Canadians write the
zip codes that indicate their postal zones?

An ABC book is a fun way to learn, no matter what topic you choose. It is a
natural way for your students (no matter what grade level) to write and draw their
knowledge and share that knowledge with someone else. At first glance, it's not a
lesson that draws on higher order thinking skills. However, the ABC approach does
allow your students' minds to rove widely and gather the fragments of information
needed to give factual substance to "in-depth" discussions. As you and your
students visit Canada on the Internet, many opportunities will arise for a
discussion of what all this information means.

Notes

Chapter 15

Get a Job!

One of the benefits of an education is that it can help you get a job. A step toward getting a job is writing a résumé. The Internet is a great resource for finding everything you need to know about conceiving and writing a résumé; finding a job; interviewing; and selling yourself personally and professionally.

With its ever-growing resources, the Internet is also an ideal place for young people to research what careers they'd like to pursue and to find the college of their choice. Almost every college has a home page on the Net for high school students to explore. A simple search will select scores of college sites.

In this chapter, you'll learn how to guide high school seniors to the various résumé home pages on the Web and then craft their own résumés in preparation for a job interview. The résumé can be for a job right now or part of an application for college. Either way, résumé writing is a skill that every student needs upon graduation and for the rest of their working lives.

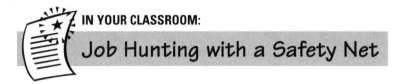

IN YOUR CLASSROOM:

Job Hunting with a Safety Net

Goal

Understand résumé development to craft a persuasive, effective résumé.

Rationale

Writing a powerful résumé is one of the first steps toward finding the job. Every professional needs to keep his or her résumé up to date because in today's world of unstable employment, you never know when you're going to need it. Practice in résumé writing will help high school students learn what it takes to produce a résumé that gets the job done right and gets a job.

Objectives

- Surf the Web to locate some home pages about résumé writing.

- Search and locate home pages where people have posted their résumés.

- Develop a résumé based on background and experience while using tips from the résumé experts on the Internet.

- Use the résumé in an interview improvisation situation.

Procedures

Set the stage by showing your students a variety of résumés. Some of the résumés should be very good and some should be just the opposite. Discuss the aspects of each type of résumé. There are many résumés on the Web, so samples are easy to find.

How to Find Résumés on the Web

The first step is to use a Web search engine, like WebCrawler or InfoSeek, to search for words like "resume," "resume writing," "curriculum vitae," or

"vita," and see what you get. Or you can do a Veronica search in gopher using the same search strategy. Each week, new sources are put on the Net and old sources are upgraded.

Tell your students that they must develop résumés that will help them get jobs or help them with their college applications. Show them various sites on the Internet that help with résumé development. Let your kids visit the résumé sites and glean the information offered there. The final product is each student's design of an honest, workable, effective résumé that he or she can use to find a job or as part of a college application or application for a scholarship, loan, or grant.

Evaluation

The final product is the proof of the lesson. Are the résumés honest, workable documents? Will they be effectual in the eyes of a prospective employer or an admissions officer? Are they attractive as well as useful? Get some parents involved who have experience in the business world or in higher education admissions. Ask them to look at drafts of the résumés, make comments and offer suggestions. When the résumés are ready, invite a couple of parents to your class to stage mock interviews with your students based on their résumés.

Listed below are Web sites where your students will find useful information about résumé writing. A few sources are for high school students, but some sources are specifically for college students and professionals. These are links your students can use when developing ideas for their own résumés.

Internet Help with Résumé Writing

Anatomy of a Résumé

URL: http://www.espan.com/docs/anatres.html

This Web site defines the basic components of a professional résumé: objective, summary of background information, skill areas, education, job history, and professional and/or community affiliations.

Joyce Lain Kennedy's Electronic Resume Writing Tips

> URL: http://www.espan.com/docs/jlkresu.html

Along with nine basic rules of résumé writing, there is some good advice, but no examples of résumés.

Important Career Information

> URL: http://www.espan.com/docs/index.html#resume

In this master list of links about how to find and keep a job, are links to résumé writing, and interviewing

Top 10 Technical Résumé writing Tips

> URL: http://www.taos.com/
> resumetips.html

Don't let the technicalities get in your way, for the ten writing tips are good ones; and they reinforce Kennedy's nine.

Top Secrets of Resume Writing

> URL: http://amsquare.com/america/advance2.html

Lots of secrets are revealed on how to make a résumé shine.

A Guide to Effective Resume Writing

> URL: http://www.ceweekly.wa.com/
> helpful/grw.html

This site provides guidance on how to write, typeset, and deliver a résumé.

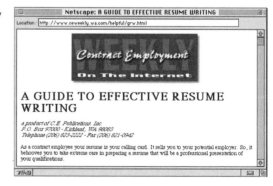

It's easier for beginners to visualize their own résumés after they have seen some samples. Not many high school kids are seeking jobs over the Internet, so there are not many résumés by teenagers posted on individual home pages. Hundreds of résumés, however, have been posted on the Internet by college students, both undergraduates and graduates. These offer excellent sources of form and substance, both good and bad. For a look at some of the résumés, open the following URLs:

Employer Directed Resume Search

 URL: http://cmc.www.drexel.edu/Drex_res/Directories/
   Interest_directory.html

College Resume Pages

 URL: http://cmc.www.drexel.edu/
   otherPages.html

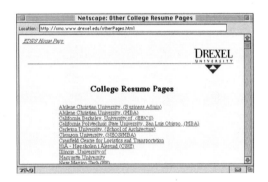

One place to publish résumés on the Web is:

Resume Database

 URL: http://rohan.sdsu.edu/home/nsbe/mosaic/resume.html

Log on to the page and follow the directions: Dialogue boxes ask for input, and after each box is filled, the user can upload that information to the Web with a simple keystroke. This is also a good site to view an outline of a résumé.

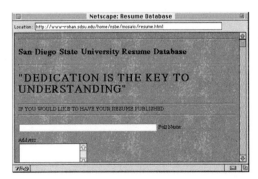

Creating a Résumé

Once students have composed their résumés based on examples and advice given from various Web sites, they need to create a neat, final version using a word-processing program. They may want to save it in two formats: as a plain text file for emailing or posting to the Web, and as a word processing file that will retain all of their font selections and formatting. This will lead to good experience at designing a résumé that is attractive and useful.

A résumé that is maintained in a computer file can be updated easily — a never-ending task. When your students get another job or finish another class or accomplish something else they are proud of, they can easily add their accomplishments to their résumés.

The résumé-writing pros all say that a résumé needs to be tailored to each job opportunity to meet the conditions and opportunities of a job offering. It's the same with a college application. A generic résumé — one size fits all — is bad strategy. Tailoring your résumé on a word processor is a piece of cake.

A résumé is a personal advertisement. It needs to be proofread by colleagues and friends before it is posted to see if it conveys the message it is supposed to convey. Résumé writing is, therefore, a high-interest opportunity for group collaboration as your students read and critique each other's résumés, making comments about how to make one another's self-ads more effective.

A final word about good taste in public: You will quickly note that many personal home pages on the Web and some résumés seem to be written without much thought as to what others may think about them. Before posting a home page or résumé on the Web, let it rest a day or two, then reread it and check to see that it says what you want it to say. Resist the urge to post items that show anger, embarrassment, or self doubt. If your home page is not ready to post, then don't post it yet. Post it only when it is ready. Call your students' attention to these blemishes in other people's self-ads, and engage your people in a discussion of how to put one's best foot forward in a global, public display of one's life, accomplishments, and talents. A home page or résumé does not have to be boring or dull, but it does need to be professional looking and positive.

Chapter 16

A Book an Hour

Teaching strategies take on a new life when adapted for use with the Internet. With this chapter, you and your students can practice using a Web browser and gopher while reading a book in an hour. "A Book an Hour" is an excellent and speedy way to introduce or read a whole book, even a literary classic, with middle and high school students.

The pre-hi-tech approach with this strategy has been the following:

- Divide a book into chapters or sections so that small groups of students can read the parts and collaborate in preparing summaries.

- Near the end of the class period, a spokesperson for each group, beginning with the group that has read the first segment of the book, tells that group's summary, and so on until the whole story had been told to the class.

- As the summaries are read, develop a master chart either on the board or an overhead transparency to map out the story according to the summaries.

- At the end, the whole class works on a summary of summaries based on the summaries of the several parts.

Together, your class will have read, reported, and summarized a whole literary classic in a single period, if the book is not too long. When I've used this approach, I've found that I needed a minimum of two class periods for the strategy to work best. I also need more time when I use the strategy with a class for the first time. Although this approach does not allow for a close reading of the text, it is a quick and easy way to introduce good literature to your students. They will get the idea that "good literature" can also be interesting and need not be tedious in the reading. This hors-d'oeuvres approach will whet their appetites for more reading on their own.

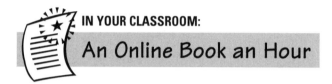

IN YOUR CLASSROOM:

An Online Book an Hour

An electronic version of "a book an hour" might go something like this: Instead of dividing up hard copy into chapters or sections, your students search out, download and divvy up, and read an electronic copy of their respective parts. If the book is not too long and is accessible online, students can read their sections directly from the Internet, but I don't recommend that: No point in tying up the connection that long.

It's more logical and less expensive to download the book onto a hard drive or diskette, convert it to the class word-processing package, divide the text into segments with block-and-copy moves, and then have your students read their segments on their computers. This way, fewer paperbooks will have to die, torn asunder; every student gets to read his or her own copy; and, at the end, a saved back-up copy of the whole book becomes the readable property of every student, the first volume in their electronic library.

While your students are reading their sections of the book on their computer screens, they can be taking notes, whether by using the comment-box mechanism or merely by opening up space between lines. Recording their thoughts instantly and easily, they can build their summaries as they read. Printed paper books, even with the widest of margins, do not allow for this extent of editorializing.

Using the block-and-move function and the split-screen, your students can assemble their electronic notes into a draft of a summary, rewrite, and reformat it with word-processing ease, and then swap disks. Each member of the group can read the draft-summaries of all the other members, typing out comments in shared-journal fashion. Then, when they meet in their groups to talk over the details and polish a final summary of that group's segment, they will have the benefit of already having read one another's individual comments and summaries.

Goal

Your students will become familiar with a classic work of literature by reading, commenting, summarizing, and crafting a summary of summaries of the selection, in one or two class periods.

Rationale

Because it is sometimes difficult to generate interest in "the dead poets" and authors whose literary legacy is a major part of the culture of our society, an electronic upgrade of their works makes them lively and readable. When our students become familiar with these fine and enjoyable works of literary art in a meaningful yet "painless" way (and at the warp-speed of a video game), then fewer of them will register the universal complaint: "This is boring!" They will be encouraged to read other classics on their own.

Objectives

- Download a work of classic literature using gopher, ftp, or a Web browser.

- Work in small groups to read, comment, and summarize a segment of the book.

- Each group member reads the others' individual summaries; they discuss and prepare a common summary of their segment.

- The whole class collaborates in reading the whole piece of good literature, and they work together to achieve understanding.

Optional Objective:

Publish a Class Illustrated Classic Comics

Students draw (either freehand or using a computer draw program) pictures for each summary. Make a notebook of the pictures, each picture to be accompanied by its respective summary, with the summary of all to complete the project. Your students can then read the written and pictorial accounts of their work.

 IN YOUR CLASSROOM:

Electronic Comparative Literature

After several books have been read using these electronic strategies, students can compare and discuss the various works of classic literature in relation to each other.

Procedures

- To generate enthusiasm, you need to stage the first event well. If you hook up with a smooth Internet connection and high-interest electronic books the first time you use the strategy, then you will be off to a good start. If you are studying the Romantic Period, for example, you will definitely want your students to read the works of Edgar Allan Poe. Show your class that you have only a few copies of the book, but thanks to the electronic age, everyone is going to read chapters of this book and make their own contributions.

- At this point, you and they surf to Poe (you will already have located the site because you want this lesson to go rapidly), and your students take it from there.

- There are several places on the Internet where the complete works of Poe are available:

Works by E.A. Poe

URL: http://bau2.uibk.ac.at/sg/poe/Work-alphabetical.html

Incomplete Online Works
of Edgar Allan Poe

URL: http://infoweb.magi.com/
~forrest/works.html

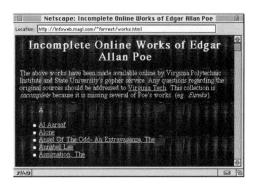

- Select the Poe title you want.
  Have your students block and copy the
  book and divide the chapters or pieces
  and copy onto diskettes for reading and
  annotating. If you have plenty of computers, your students can work alone
  or in pairs. If you have more students than you have computers, then each
  group of three or four students can cluster around a computer. Let one
  student act as electronic scribe, seated at the keyboard, while the others in
  the group read the screen and offer comments.

- As a regular routine in English or Language Arts class, this strategy can be
  used about once every other week quite effectively. Students enjoy it and
  look forward to doing it again and again. You may assign your students to do
  the surfing to find next week's book.

Evaluation

The various possible versions of this activity are easy to evaluate: Did the
chapter/segment summary-writing work? Did your students take hold of
their parts of the book and inwardly digest them? Did the summary of
summaries work — is it logical and accurate? Is there a notebook of
summaries and the summary of summaries? How does the homegrown
Illustrated Comic Classic look? Above all, did your students engage
wholeheartedly in the discussion of the book? If you can answer yes to these
questions, you and your students did a good job.

Many sources for classic literature are available on the Internet. Below you
see a list of a few of them from both GopherSpace and the Web. Use
directories or search engines to generate your own list: Search under
"Literature," the names of your favorite authors, or even topics.
The addresses do work, but oftentimes, if you have not subscribed to the
service, you cannot download the documents. For this reason, you will want

to have crawled around the Web in search of free, downloadable literature, or be ready to pay.

Especially the first time you try this strategy, you want to make sure that your goal is attainable. By assigning the Internet search-work to your students for next time, they will learn how to find electronic literature for themselves. You can go to the Online Library at:

URL: gopher://wiretap.spies.com:70/11/Library/Classic

There you can view links to many titles. If the chapter or section is too long, your browser will ask you where you want the chapter saved. This is when I put things on a diskette. Downloading information takes a lot of room on a hard drive.

Whole books on the Internet

The Electronic Text Center at the University of Virginia

URL: http://etext.lib.virginia.edu/ english.html

This list includes hyperlinks to several hundred books written in English, and at the main site (http://etext.lib.virginia.edu/ uvaonline.html) you can read books in French, German, Japanese, or Latin.

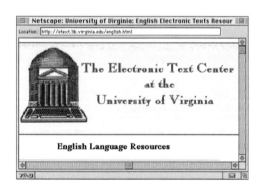

Books On-line By Title

URL: http://www-cgi.cs.cmu.edu/cgi-bin/book/maketitlepage

Maintained by the library at Carnegie Mellon University, this is a general collection of literary works organized by title.

ALEX: A Catalog of Electronic Texts

   URL: gopher://vega.lib.ncsu.edu:70/11/library/stacks/Alex

This gopher list has many complete works, searchable by author, subject or title.

The Online Book Initiative

   URL: gopher://gopher.std.com/

In your browser, type this gopher address, then click on OBI, the Online Book Initiative to view a list of over 150 authors and categories. There are books by G. Chaucer and E. Brontë, by Edgar Allan Poe and Sir Arthur Conan Doyle, from Anglo-Saxon literature to Samuel Clemens, etc.

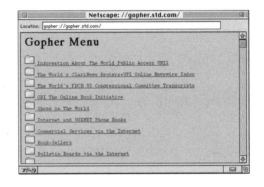

There are other things here, too: weather maps, speeches by President Clinton, and Star Trek stories. You will be surprised at all there is to read at this one location. With this one site, you will never lack for literature.

The Bard on the Internet

   URL: http://the-tech.mit.edu/Shakespeare/works.html

The works of William Shakespeare are read by most tenth, eleventh, and twelfth grade classes. The full text of Shakespeare's plays, poems, and sonnets can be downloaded from the University of Minnesota gopher. The collection is arranged by category: comedy, history, poetry, tragedy, etc.

Women and Literature

   URL: http://sunsite.unc.edu/cheryb/women/wlit.html

If your class is interested in women writers, you can find short biographical sketches and some of the works of Louisa May Alcott, Jane Austen, Emily Brontë, and Sylvia Plath, among others.

Victorian Women Writers

> URL: http://www.indiana.edu/~letrs/vwwp/

A collection of 37 works by 12 British writers in the Victorian Era.

A Celebration of Women Writers

> URL: http://www.cs.cmu.edu/Web/People/mmbt/women/writers.html

A list of women authors with either biographies or their writings.

Download to your heart's content! Most of it is all still free for the taking — it's like being given an unlimited gift certificate to your favorite bookstore. You will need to establish a storage policy for your class because those hard drives will fill up in no time. If your system includes a spacious server, and every user has a "student locker" in which to save downloaded files, then you are lucky. If not, it's every kid with a floppy for him- or herself.

"A Book An Hour" with your own adaptations is a favorite strategy among whole language teachers, English teachers, and plugged-in, turned-on book lovers. As a library that never closes, that doesn't require you to return the books, and levies no fines, the Internet is the greatest!

Chapter 17

Just for the Little Kids

A colleague of mine has a seven-year-old and a 23-month-old. The seven-year-old is already a computer whiz: He plays games, does his own Net searches for more games, is knowledgeable about both hardware and software, and has even started doing homework on the family computer. His little brother had mostly been watching.

One hot day, when mother and sons came home from a grocery-shopping expedition, the 23-month-old imperiously commanded: "Puter, Mommy! Puter!" "In a minute, honey!" my friend replied, wiping the melting ice cream off her elbow.

Impatient, the younger sibling scrambled up the stairs to the computer room, and in a few seconds, my friend heard the "Ding!" that told her that someone had turned on the computer. "He can't hurt it or himself," she thought, and finished putting the groceries away, and then forgot all about it. Thirty minutes later, she remembered — stillness in a house full of kids is a loud warning. Up the stairs she went.

The toddler had turned on the switch at the surge blocker, negotiated the main menu, found the game he wanted, and was now blissfully wrapped up in 'puter play.

What 3-4-5-6-7-8-year-olds Can Do with the Internet

How young can they learn? It's a question of motor control, not of mind — the mind is ready to learn at birth. For teachers, the point is this: Your kids are probably already inherently better at 'puters than you are because they are younger, naturally meddlesome, full of curiosity, and many of them grew up with these machines.

More important, kids' minds are like a whole roll of expensive paper towels: They can soak up almost as much as you can pour on them, and at an early age. Have no hesitation about presenting sophisticated Internet instruction to even your youngest students. What they can't execute on their own, they can watch and learn from. They can understand just about anything you tell them, if you use words that they know.

The Internet is full of links and ideas for 3-4-5-6-7-and-8-year-olds: stories, games, pictures, and just the sheer fascination of watching the world blip and bleep on a screen before their eyes. Just as Sesame Street gave a whole generation a head start with reading readiness, kids raised by computer games are going to be ahead with a variety of skills: small motor control, hierarchical logic (finding their way along paths and down menus), spelling (one has to be precise when keying in http addresses), and keyboard writing readiness (it's easier to type than it is to wield a pen or pencil).

Little people can surf the Internet, drive the engines, download the files, and play the games just like big people, though they may need a bit more help. You probably will not have all your little people working with the Internet on a daily basis, but my guess is that you will find them eager to log on. As the story of my friend and her toddler indicates, kids and 'puters are natural allies. If you have a computer in your classroom, there's no reason for it not to be used by someone all the time. Getting some of them to leave it alone will be a bigger problem than getting most of them interested in it! So, even in kindergarten and the primary grades, make the Internet an integral part of your curriculum. It can teach so much and with so little effort or stress.

One problem you will confront is the age-old problem of the have's and the have-not's. Some young kids have computers at home, and they will come to your class already computer literate and ready to turn on and log in. Others not only will not have computers at home but also they will never have even touched a computer keyboard. In our time, the computer have-not's are seriously at risk in the scramble for knowledge, and it is your job as a teacher to help make computer equality a new amendment to the Constitution.

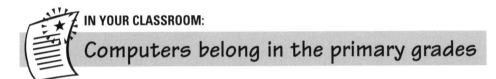

IN YOUR CLASSROOM:

Computers belong in the primary grades

Right now, I'm seeing lots of kindergartners coming to school who already know how to operate a computer. They can turn it on and off, identify letters on the keyboard, and use rudimentary hunt-and-peck typing skills to access and work on the programs that they know. Your students who have this much skill can also access the Internet. Your other students will need your help to catch up, but they will catch up fast.

The computer is an excellent resource for teaching left-to-right reading orientation (a desperately needed corrective against the evil effects of watching too much television), symbol-to-letter recognition, sound-to-symbol recognition, and word-to-symbol recognition. On the other hand, not all grownups like computers, and neither do all kids.

Children whose "frame of mind" is dominantly bodily-kinesthetic (as Howard Gardner might put it) may have trouble sitting still for computer time. Let's not make the mistake that has been made so often in the past: This new technology is not as appealing to some as it is to others, and it will not work equally well for all. Let's not persecute the kids who don't like computers.

When you involve your students in an email activity, they will begin to communicate with one another on a plane quite different from the ordinary. Email gives adults instant intimacy and an ability to work together without knowing one another well. I do not know what goes on in the minds of little kids as they face a screen with a message on it from their peers, but an equally powerful mental alchemy is at work, and it is good. Minimally, the email experience seems to help little people get out of their ego-centered stage in kindergarten and first grade, so that they can start thinking about, and with, others.

Internet work is trickier with little ones, but possible. Peer collaboration is one excellent way to go. Work with a teacher in a higher grade, and set up a couple of times in the week for your little guys to work with the older kids. To make maximal use of the available computers, some of your kids could go to the other room, and some of the other kids could come to your room. With this computer-buddy system, your students can surf the Net, play computer games, read files, compose email, download programs, games, and files, carry on a keypal correspondence with someone somewhere overseas (or across town), and compose their own literary masterpieces.

See Chapter 8 for addresses of listservs that specialize in electronic penpals, even for the little guys. Here are two sites you can visit:

Kid's Com

   URL: http://www.kidscom.com//

Parents and Teachers

   URL: http://www.kidscom.com/
   parentsplace.html

In addition to those sites, take a look at the email books these second graders are publishing at Hoffer Elementary School and Murphy Ranch School. Both are accessible at: http://cmp1.ucr.edu/exhibitions/hoffer/home/hoffer.e-mail.html

In situations where the younger students have text in their heads but insufficient skills to write them down, the older students can do the writing or typing. Taking dictation from the younger buddy is good writing practice for the older buddy, and, then, reading the print-out will prove to be an altogether inspiring "language-experience" literacy event for the young author.

This approach is good for both sets of kids for more reasons than just teaching them computer skills. The bigger kids learn about patience, along with listening, asking, clarifying, helping, and giving feedback, not to mention typing, spelling, grammar, and reading skills. (Reassure your young peer tutors that they can ask you for help, if they get stuck.) The littler kids learn how to compose their thoughts and dictate them in a logical manner, how to answer questions intelligently, how to correct an older person thoughtfully, and how rationally to get what they want. Both kinds of kids learn how to get along with one another.

After your students have worked with email and are comfortable with their cyberbuddies, they can venture out onto the Internet together. At first, I thought ftp was too difficult for six-year-olds. That notion lasted until I saw home pages that had been made by young children! These youngsters have set up home pages comprising their own stuff plus documents from all over the Internet.

PeanutNet

There are many home pages on the Web authored by kids or their parents. It's difficult to tell who is doing the coding. However, Internet resources are read, point, and click interfaces, so they are not technologically difficult for youngsters to access. Good Web browsers have graphics and sound capabilities that make them ideal for younger kids. Computers equipped with audio programs and sound cards and video capacities make the Web just that much more appealing to kids. Many of the home pages created by the kids have sound and quick time movies, and all of them have links to other Web sites. Here are a couple of the many home pages created by or for little people.

David's Home Page

URL: http://www.charm.net/
~jcain/david.html

The author is five years old, he loves snakes and he is a home schooler.

Emma Bowen's Home Page

> URL: http://www.comlab.ox.ac.uk/oucl/users/jonathan.bowen/children/emma.html

Emma is eight years old, she lives in Oxford, England, and her daddy "plays with computers."

Kids Did This

> URL: http://sln.fi.edu/tfi/hotlists/kids.html

This hot link collection of kid-generated stuff starts out with this warning: "It's a challenge to keep up with kids on the Internet, but we're trying. Our hotlist of student-produced stuff became too long for one page! Explore the topics that interest you. One word of caution: Some student-designed pages take extra time to load. Caveat surfer."

Kids Space

> URL: http://www.interport.net/kids-space/

You can read stories written by kids, view their paintings, ask a doctor for advice, or switch languages from English to Japanese. The youthful authors proclaim their "page is rated G," and it is.

Internet for Little Guys

The Web is icon-oriented, which makes pointing and clicking easy for beginners. If you have some bookmarks to sites of high interest already loaded, that will make the process easier still. Many home pages are quite graphical, with pictures and brief explanations that are self-explanatory.

Theodore Tugboat

    URL: http://www.cochran.com/tt.html

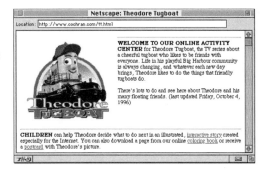

This comprehensive and fun home page of a Canadian television program is new every day, and you do not need to have seen the TV program for the activities to make sense. Kids love the interactive storybook with pictures, the coloring book, and the hot links for kids to other places they like to go on the Internet.

Timmy the Tooth

    URL: http://www.mca.com/home/playroom/cgi-bin/story/timmy

To personalize this interactive story, your child can write his or her name in a box.

Mac Colouring Book

    URL: http://www.simcoe.net/karen/coloring.htm

If you want to see another coloring book, here are pages you can download and color.

Carlos' Coloring Book

    URL: http://www.ravenna.com/coloring/

One of the first coloring books on the Web, I've tried to use it, but it never works for me. I've seen kids use it, and it works every time. I guess you just have to be a kid!

Alex's Scribbles — Koala Trouble

> URL: http://www.peg.apc.org/~balson/story/

The idea for the story Koala Trouble is by Alex, a five year old, but the Web page is done by his dad. This is a clever story.

Children's Stories on the Web

Not all Web sites are written by children, some are written for children. There are many Web sites that feature children's literature, and I've only listed a few. Luckily, each of these Web sites has links to other sources of online children's literature.

Children's Story Books Online

> URL: http://www.magickeys.com/books/

Possibly the best of the story sites on the Web.

Storybook Land

> URL: http://members.gnn.com/shickman/main.htm

With the links to many children's book online you can go to the Oz books, general resources for children's literature, fairy tales, and so much more.

The IPL Story Hour

> URL: http://ipl.sils.umich.edu/youth/StoryHour/

Part of the Internet Public Library Web site, it has links to several stories you can read aloud to your kids. You might want to check out the main index for the youth IPL at http://ipl.sils.umich.edu/youth/index.html

Internet Favorites of Kids

Since even before Jurassic Park and Barney, dinosaurs have long been a favorite of most primary students. On several lists of "kids' favorites" and "what's cool for kids," is:

The Dinosaur Tour at the Field Museum
    URL: http://www.bvis.uic.edu/museum/exhibits/dino/Triassic.html

It is informative and interesting, with text and graphics. Check it out and judge for yourself whether it's right for your kids. If you decide to teach your primary students using the Dinosaur Homepage, I'd be curious to know how it went. Send some e-mail to ecotton@oavax.csuchico.edu

Besides big things like dinosaurs, little kids also like small wiggly things.

The Froggy Page
    URL: http://www.cs.yale.edu/homes/sjl/froggy.html

It's just right for certain kinds of pro-green primary kids. This home page has links to scads of frog-type documents, graphics, fun things to do, and even coloring pages. If you want to delight your six-, seven-, and eight-year-old herpetologists, click and point them to The Froggy Page.

Explore the Internet with Dr. I
    URL: http://ipl.sils.umich.edu/
        youth/DrInternet/

A great site for science-minded kids who want to know more about dinosaurs, volcanoes, weather, earthquakes, space, and other cool sites, Dr. I is part of the Internet Public Library.

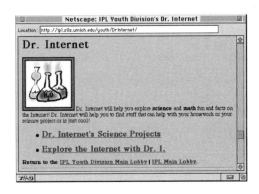

The International Museum of the Horse

URL: http://www.horseworld.com/imhmain.html

I would be remiss if I did not mention this Web site. It has links to information about horses, and young horse lovers think it's great!

A Site for Kids and Parents Together

Parents and Children Together are read-along stories for parents (or teachers) and kids, ages 4-10, and can be found at the Web site of the ERIC Clearinghouse on Reading, English, and Communication (ERIC/REC) at http://www.indiana.edu/~eric_rec/fl/ras.html

Several stories are available already, and the ERIC folk have three years' worth of monthly read-along stories that they are aiming to put online. Soon, the stories will be accompanied by online audio narration.

Quick and Easy Ways to Get Your Kids Published on the Web

Because the archival capacity of virtual space on the Internet is practically infinite, all the old constraints and cautions of the hard-copy publishing world are out-moded. Now, everyone who wants to can get published electronically. If you can't find a place that looks just right to place your electronic publications, you can set up your own electronic publishing company by merely saying so on your own home page. Your class can set up its own home page (see Chapter 5, "Developing and Designing Web Pages") and publish whatever you and your students like. If you and your class go into the publishing business, you will want to do so with the backing of your principal. Schools are accountable for the electronic publications of their students, just as they are for other kinds of school publications. So I advise you to take advantage of the wisdom of the ages collected in school journalism guides. Here are to two existing sites where your kids are welcome to publish their own stories, and where they can read stories published by other kids.

KidsPub

　　URL: http://www.en-garde.com/kidpub/

Here's a world-wide interactive story to which your kids are invited to add their own paragraphs. You and your students can see what other kids are doing in school. Encouraging and empowering, KidsPub is proof that little people can and do write good stories and get them published.

Put My Story on the WWW

　　URL: http://ipl.sils.umich.edu/youth/PutMyStory/

Yet another link of the Internet Public Library project, read stories written by kids from four to fourteen years old.

Home Schoolers on the Web

　　The Internet is also useful for home schoolers. There are many Web sites for home schoolers; take a look at just a few of them. Each has links to other home school Web sites, so you should not have any trouble finding things for your kids to do on the Internet. By the way, there are some good links for children on these pages, too.

The Home School Page

　　URL: http://www.alaska.net/~mteel/homesch/homeschl.html

Part of a larger page by the Teel Family of Alaska, to see their page, click on http://www.alaska.net/~mteel/index.html

Cain Hotlist

　　URL: http://www.charm.net/~jcain/hotlist.html#Home Schooling

A list of links to about twenty home school pages on the Internet

Internet Educational Resources

　　URL: http://www.cts.com/~netsales/herc/hercoir.htm

A Web site developed by the Home Education Resources Center, it has links for kids that are both fun and educational.

Time to Get Going

Other sites besides these are available for young kids, but we could use many more such sites. This is a ripe opportunity for you and your class to take on the project of developing your own home page, going into the electronic publishing business, and linking up with anything that interests your 3-4-5-6-7-8-year-old students. Cyber-buddies, older with younger, can collaborate to design, code, test, and upload a school home page with individual home pages for each of the grades or for the several rooms. See chapter 5 to get started on your own home page.

So much is possible by way of using the Internet to teach and learn:

• Read and discuss on e-mail electronic books, linking your class with one down the hall, across town, or on the other side of the globe.

• Go to The Froggy Page for ideas, and cross-reference to develop a lesson by linking to frog fables and frog stories on other pages. All these references can be integrated by linking to yet another page about frog habitat, which can be given a scientific bent by linking to the Virtual Frog Dissection Kit (if you have the stomach for that sort of thing). With this kind of electronic leap-frogging, you could hot link an excellent Frog Unit together!

• Go to the Internet Public Library and see a kitchen science experiment by Dr. I(nternet); then see if it will work in your classroom.

As with every other chapter in this book, I would thoroughly appreciate your feedback and suggestions. Please help me build my online course on how to teach, using the Internet! Have you found any other good Web sites for computer whizzes in the twenty-three-month-old to K through primary range? I'd love to hear from you-e-mail: ecotton@oavax.csuchico.edu Thank you!

Appendix A

Selected Internet Books

Ackermann, Ernest C. (1995).
Learning to Use the Internet: An Introduction With Examples and Exercises.
Wilsonville, Oregon: Franklin Beedle & Associates. ($17.00, ISBN: 0938661922)

Ahmad, Nyla, Martha Newbigging, and Keltie Thomas (1996).
Cybersurfer: The Owl Internet Guide for Kids. Book and Disk.
Toronto: Owl Communications. ($19.95, ISBN: 1895688507)

Barron, Ann (1996).
Teaching with the Web: HTML for Teachers
Lancaster, PA: Wentworth Worldwide Media ($39.95, ISBN: 932577-43-1)

Bauer, David G. (1996).
Educators' Internet Funding Guide.
Lancaster, PA: Wentworth Worldwide Media and Upper Saddle River, NJ:
Prentice Hall. ($44.94, ISBN: 0-13-569492-2)

Benson, Allen C., and Linda Fodemski (1996).
Connecting Kids and the Internet:
   A Handbook for Librarians, Teachers and Parents
(Neal-Schuman Net-Guide Series). New York: Neal Schuman Publications.
($35.00, ISBN: 1555702449)

Biggar, Bill, and Joe Myers (1996).
Danger Zones: What Parents Should Know About the Internet.
Kansas City: Andrews & McMeel. ($10.95, ISBN: 0836213173)

Breeding, Marshall, ed. (1995).
Mecklermedia's Official Internet World: World Wide Web Yellow Pages 1996.
Book and CD-ROM Edition. Foster City, California: IDG Books Worldwide.
($39.99, ISBN: 1568843445)

Burke, John (1996).
Learning the Internet: A Workbook for Beginners
(Neal Schuman Net-Guide Series). New York: Neal Schuman Publications.
($29.95, ISBN: 1555702481)

Castro, Elizabeth (1996).
HTML: For the World Wide Web
(Visual Quickstart Guide). Berkeley, California: Peachpit Press. ($17.95, ISBN: 0201884488)

Clark, Carol Lea (1996).
A Student's Guide to the Internet.
Upper Saddle River, New Jersey: Prentice Hall. ($17.40, ISBN: 0134423100)

Crispin, Patrick Douglas, and Mark D. Ciampa (1996).
Atlas for the Information Superhighway.
Cincinnati: South-Western Publishing Company. ($34.25, ISBN: 0538658649)

Crumlish, Christian (1966).
The ABCs of the Internet.
San Francisco: Sybex. ($19.99, ISBN: 0782118879)

December, John, and Neil Randall (1996).
The World Wide Web Unleashed 1996.
Indianapolis: Sams Publishing Company. ($49.99, ISBN: 1575210401)

Distefano, Vince (1996).
Child Safety on the Internet.
Lancaster, PA: Wentworth Worldwide Media and Upper Saddle River, NJ: Prentice Hall.
($34.95, ISBN: 0-13-569568-X)

Ellsworth, Jill H. (1994).
Education on the Internet: A Hands-on Book of Ideas, Resources, Projects, and Advice.
Indianapolis: Sams Publishing Company. ($25.00, ISBN: 0-067-30595-X)

Frazier, Deneen, Barbara Kurshan, and Sara Armstrong (1995).
Internet for Kids.
Book and Disk. San Francisco: Sybex. ($22.99, ISBN: 0782117414)

Garfield, Gary M., and Suzanne McDonough (1995).
Modems, Megabytes and Me: Telecommunicating Across the Curriculum.
Winnipeg, Manitoba, Canada: Pegius Publishers.
($16.00, ISBN: 1-895411-78-5)

Giagnocavo, Gregory, Tim McLain, and Chris Sturm (1996).
Educator's Internet Companion
Lancaster, PA: Wentworth Worldwide Media. Book, CD-ROM, and Video.
($39.95, ISBN: 0-932577-10-5)

Giagnocavo, Gregory, ed. (1995).
Educator's World Wide Web Tourguide:
  Classroom Connect's Guide to the Best 150 Web Sites for K-12 Education.
Lancaster, Pennsylvania: Wentworth Publications. Book and CD-ROM.
($39.95, ISBN: 0932577164)

Glister, Paul (1996).
    Finding It on the Internet: The Internet Navigator's Guide to Search Tools and Techniques.
    New York: John Wiley & Sons. ($24.95, ISBN: 0471126950)

Glossbrenner, Alfred, Emily Glossbrenner, and John Grimes (illustrator) (1996).
    The Little Web Book.
    Berkeley, California: Peachpit Press. ($14.95, ISBN: 0201883678)

Hahn, Harley (1996).
    The Internet Complete Reference.
    Second Edition. New York: Osborne McGraw-Hill. ($32.95, ISBN: 007882138X)

Harris, Judi (1994).
    Way of the Ferret: Finding Educational Resources on the Internet.
    Revised Edition. Eugene, Oregon: International Society for Technology in Education.
    ($24.95, ISBN: 0-68-5727-62-9)

Junor, Bill, and Chris Demontravel (1995).
    Internet: The User's Guide for Everyone.
    Boston: Branden Publishing Company. ($16.95, ISBN: 0828320136)

Laquey, Tracey (1994).
    The Internet Companion: A Beginner's Guide to Global Networking.
    Reading, Massachusetts: Addison-Wesley Publishing Company. ($12.95, ISBN: 0201407663)

Mautner, Chris and Chris Sturm (1996).
    Family Internet Companion.
    Lancaster, PA: Wentworth Worldwide Media and Upper Saddle River, NJ: Prentice Hall.
    Book and CD-ROM. ($39.95, ISBN: 0-13-569500-7)

McLain, Tim (1996).
    Internet Homework Helper.
    Lancaster, PA: Wentworth Worldwide Media and Upper Saddle River, NJ: Prentice Hall.
    Book and CD-ROM. ($29.95, ISBN: 0-13-259557-5)

Nelson, Stephen L. (1995).
    Field Guide to the Internet.
    Redmond, Washington: Microsoft Press. ($8.95, ISBN: 155615822X)

Nelson, Stephen L. (1996).
    The World Wide Web for Busy People.
    New York: Osborne McGraw-Hill. ($22.95, ISBN: 0078822440)

Peal, David (1995).
    Access the Internet!
    San Francisco: Sybex. ($22.99, ISBN: 0782117449)

Pedersen, Ted, and Francis Moss (1995).
Internet for Kids!: A Beginner's Guide to Surfing the Net.
New York: Price Stern Sloan Publishers. ($8.95, ISBN: 0843139579)

Place, Ron, Klaus Dimmler, Thomas Powell, and Ron Chapman (1996).
Educator's Internet Yellow Pages.
Upper Saddle River, New Jersey: Prentice Hall Computer Books.
($26.95, ISBN: 0132323567)

Polly, Jean Armour (1996).
The Internet Kids Yellow Pages.
International Edition. New York: Osborne McGraw-Hill. ($19.95)

Pomeroy, Brian (1996).
Beginnernet : A Beginner's Guide to the Internet and the World Wide Web.
Second Edition. Thorofare, New Jersey: Slack. ($18.95, ISBN: 1556423225)

Rankin, Bob (1996).
Dr. Bob's Painless Guide to the Internet & Amazing Things You Can Do with E-Mail.
Daly City, California: No Starch Press. ($12.95, ISBN: 1886411093)

Schepp, Debra, and Brad Schepp (1995).
Kidnet: The Kid's Guide to Surfing through Cyberspace.
New York: HarperCollins. ($14.00, ISBN: 006273380X)

Smith, Richard J., Mark Gibbs, and Paul McFedries (1995).
Navigating the Internet.
Third Edition. Indianapolis: Samsnet. ($22.50, ISBN: 0672307189)

Steen, Douglas R., Mark R. Roddy, Derek Sheffield, and Michael Bryan Stout (1995).
Teaching with the Internet: Putting Teachers before Technology.
Bellevue, Washington: Resolution Business Press. ($16.95, ISBN 0-945264-19-4)

Strudwick, Karen, John Spilker, and Jay Arney (1996).
Internet for Parents.
Bellevue, Washington: Resolution Business Press. ($24.95, ISBN 0-945264-17-8)

Vitanza, Victor J. (1996).
Cyberreader.
Boston: Allyn & Bacon. ($27.95, ISBN: 0205197795)

Wiggins, Richard (1994).
The Internet for Everyone: A Guide for Users and Providers.
New York: McGraw-Hill. (ISBN: 0-07-067019-6)

Williams, Bard (1995).
The Internet for Teachers.
Book and Disk. Foster City, California: IDG Books Worldwide. ($19.99, ISBN: 1568846002)

Appendix B

Glossary

Acceptable Use Policy (AUP)

A binding document signed by all users that explains the rules of Internet use at an institution.

Anonymous ftp

A publicly available Internet file site. Users must sign on as "anonymous" and enter their email addresses to connect to an anonymous ftp site.

Archie

A program that locates files that are freely available on anonymous ftp sites across the Internet. To use Archie, telnet to one of these sites and logon as archie.

archie.internic.net
archie.ans.net
archie.rutgers.edu
archie.sura.net
archie.unl.edu
archie.au
archie.doc.ic.ac.uk

Type **help** to obtain full instructions.

Bitnet

An autonomous network of academic and research sites.

Browser

Software that allows users to access and navigate the World Wide Web. Some Web browsers, such as Mosaic and NetScape, are graphical. Lynx is a text-based browser used on Unix computers.

Bulletin Board Service (BBS)

A forum for users to browse and exchange information. Computer BBSs are accessible by telephone via a personal computer and a modem. Many BBSs are small operations run by a single person that allow only several users to logon at the same time. Some are much larger and allow hundreds of users to logon simultaneously to use the system. Huge, commercial examples are America Online, CompuServe, and Prodigy.

Commercial online service

A company that, for a fee, allows computer users to dial in via modem to access its information and services, which can include Internet access. Examples are America Online, CompuServe, and Prodigy.

Database

A computer holding large amounts of information that can be searched by an Internet user. A storehouse of information on the Net.

Dialup Internet connection

Lets a user dial into an Internet service provider using a modem and telephone line to access the Internet. The user is presented with a text-based set of menus which are used to navigate the Internet. (See SLIP or PPP connections)

Directory

A list of files or other directories on a computer at an Internet site.

Download/upload

To download is to transfer a file from another computer to the user's computer. To upload is to send a file to another computer.

Email

Allows users to send and receive messages to each other over the Internet.

Emoticons

Smileys and other character art used to express feelings in email communication.

File Transfer Protocol (FTP)

Allows files to be transferred between Internet-connected computers.

Filter

Hardware or software designed to restrict access to certain areas on the Internet.

Finger

Software that allows the user to enter the address of an Internet site to find information about that system's users or a particular user. Some finger addresses return other topic-specific information.

Flame

To send a harsh, critical email message to another user, usually someone who has violated the rules of netiquette.

Free-Net

Any one of more than two dozen freely accessible Internet sites, primarily offering community and educational information.

Frequently Asked Questions (FAQ)

FAQ files answer frequently asked questions on hundreds of Internet-related topics. They're freely available at many locations on the Net. This ftp site holds every FAQ on the Net.

URL: ftp://rtfm.mit.edu

Go to the **pub/usenet/news.answers** subdirectory

Gopher

A menu-based system for browsing Internet information.

Graphical interface

Software designed to allow the user to execute commands by pointing and clicking on icons or text.

Hacker

A computer user who illegally visits networked computers to look around or cause harm.

Home page

The first page a user sees when visiting a World Wide Web site.

HTML (Hypertext Markup Language)

Programming "language" of the World Wide Web, HTML software turns a document into a hyperlinked World Wide Web page.

Hypertext/hyperlink

A highlighted word or graphic in a document that, when clicked upon, takes the user to a related piece of information on the Internet.

Infobot (or mailbot)

An email address that automatically returns information requested by the user.

Internaut

Anyone who uses the Internet.

Internet

The global "network of networks" that connects more than four million computers, called hosts. The Internet is the virtual "space" in which users send and receive email, logon to remote computers (telnet), browse databases of information (gopher, World Wide Web, WAIS), and send and receive programs (ftp) contained on these computers.

Internet account

Purchased through an Internet service provider, the account assigns a password and email address to an individual or group.

Internet Relay Chat (IRC)

Interactive, real-time discussions between Internauts using text messages. Users logon to designated Net computers and join discussions already in progress. More information about IRC can be obtained via ftp.

URL: ftp://cs.bu.edu

Go to the **irc/support** subdirectory

Internet server

A computer that stores data that can be accessed via the Internet.

Internet Service Provider (ISP)

Any organization that provides access to the Internet. Many ISPs also offer technical assistance to schools looking to become Internet information providers by placing their school's information online. They also help schools get connected to the Net. A list of ISPs can be retrieved via ftp.

URL: ftp://ftp.classroom.net

Look in the **wentworth** subdirectory

Internet site

A computer connected to the Internet containing information that can be accessed using an Internet navigation tool such as ftp, telnet, gopher, or a Web browser.

IP address

Every computer on the Internet has a unique numerical address assigned to it, such as 123.456.78.9.

Jughead

An Internet search tool that will scan one or a few gopher sites for material related to a keyword.

Keyword

A word or words which can be searched for in documents or menus.

Knowbot

Software that searches Internet "white pages," lists of users at large institutions, to find a person's name and address.

Logon

To sign on to a computer system.

Mailing lists (or Listserv)

There are more than 4,000 topic-oriented, email-based message bases that can be read and posted to. Users subscribe to the lists they want to read and receive messages via email. Mailing lists are operated using listserv software. Thus, many Internauts call mailing lists "listservers." There are two types of lists: moderated and unmoderated. Moderated lists are screened by a human before being posted to subscribers. Messages to unmoderated lists are automatically forwarded to subscribers.

Menu

A list of information that leads to documents or other menus.

Modem

An electronic device that attaches to a computer and links that computer to the online world via a phone line. Modems are available for any computer, can be internal or external, and come in several speeds, known as the baud rate. The higher the baud rate, the faster the modem. The most popular modem was 14,400 baud but 28,800 baud modems are now the standard. Most Internet service providers allow you to dial into their systems at 14,400, or even 28,800 baud.

Mosaic

Internet navigation software that allows Internauts to access information through a graphical, point-and-click interface rather than text-only screens or menus. Mosaic is known as a Web browser because it accesses World Wide Web information formatted into special home pages using hypertext. Other graphical Web browsers include NetScape, WinWeb, InternetWorks, and Cello.

National Information Infrastructure (NII)

The official U.S. government name for the Internet and other computer networks. Commonly known as the Information Superhighway.

Netiquette

The rules of conduct for Internet users. Violating netiquette could result in flaming or removal from a mailing list. Some service providers will even cancel a user's Internet account, denying him or her access to the Net, if the violation is severe enough.

Net surfer

Someone who browses the Internet.

Network

A group of computers that are connected in some fashion. Most school networks are known as LANs, or Local Area Networks, because they are networks linking computers in one small area. The Internet could be referred to as a WAN, or a Wide Area Network, because it connects computers in more than one local area.

Online/Offline

When you are logged onto a computer through your modem, you are said to be online. When you're using your computer but are not connected to a computer through your modem, you're said to be working offline.

Posts

Email messages sent to a mailing list or Usenet newsgroup to be read by subscribers or others on the Internet.

Request for Comments (RFC)

Online documents that have to do with technical standards for the Internet.

Serial Line Internet Protocol (SLIP) or
Point to Point Protocol (PPP, a Dial-up IP) Internet connections

Both allow a computer to connect to the Internet using a modem and telephone line. Users then navigate the Internet using software on their own computer. This is in contrast to using a Dialup Internet Connection, where users are forced to navigate the Net using text-based sets of menus.

Signature file

Return address information such as name, phone number, and email address that users put at the bottom of email messages.

Telnet

Allows users to access computers and their data at thousands of places around the world, most often at libraries, universities, and government agencies.

Text-based Internet account

The user must use Unix commands to navigate the Internet.

Unix

A computer operating system commonly used on the Internet.

URL (Universal Resource Locator)

The address and method used to locate a specific resource on the Internet.
A URL beginning with **http://** indicates that the site is a WWW resource and that a Web browser will access it.

Usenet newsgroups

More than 13,000 topic-oriented message bases that can be read and posted to. Also called newsgroups.

Veronica

Veronica is a computer program that helps Internauts find what they're looking for on gopher servers around the world. Instead of looking through menus, Veronica allows users to enter keywords to locate the gopher site that holds the information they want.

URL: gopher://veronica.scs.unr.edu

Virtual

A computer-generated environment.

WAIS (Wide Area Information Servers)

These servers allow users to conduct full-text keyword searches in documents, databases, and libraries connected to the Internet.

World Wide Web (WWW or Web)

A revolutionary Internet browsing system that allows for point-and-click navigation of the Internet. The WWW is a spider-web-like interconnection of millions of pieces of information located on computers around the world. Web documents use hypertext, which incorporates text and graphical "links" to other documents and files on Internet-connected computers.

Appendix

The Online Classroom CD-ROM

Here are the details about your BONUS Online Classroom CD-ROM, jam-packed with free software to get you onto the Internet and using its resources in minutes! There are the **eleven** main items on this CD:

1. Internet access software. From EarthLink Network,® this includes EarthLink Network TotalAccess™ software with Netscape Navigator™. The software entitles you to 10 days free, unlimited dial-in Internet access with no sign-up fee.

2. Online Classroom HotPage. This HTML file contains "live" Internet links to many of the best online sites listed throughout this book. Simply use your Web browser to load the **HOTPAGE.HTM** file.

3. Online Classroom text files. Includes electronic versions of all the lesson plans within this book.

4. HyperStudio™ multimedia software demo. Enables you to use the multimedia files you find on the Internet to create colorful, interactive slide shows. This demo version also includes over 150 MB of clip art, video clips, sounds, and other multimedia files.

5. Monstrous Media Kit for Macintosh.

 Multimedia authoring software that's perfect for students new to computers who want to create fun, informative interactive presentations with sounds and video.

6. CyberPatrol™ Internet access filter software.
A highly flexible and effective means for blocking
access to inappropriate online sites. This version is
enabled for a full 30-day free trial. You can purchase
the full version complete with a one year subscription to
the CyberNot list for only $29 (regularly $51).

7. Electric Library™ software. Provides an outstanding
online research collection. This version is enabled for a full
30-day free trial — a whole month's access to a complete
online research library.

8. Internet Coach 3.0 Lite. An easy-to-use, online tutorial for traveling the
Internet with your Netscape Web browser. You'll be an expert in minutes.
Full versions and site licenses available at a discount from *Classroom Connect.*

9. Internet Coach for Kids – Mission to Planet X. Made just for kids,
this multimedia online tutorial will help your youngsters learn how to use the
Internet in minutes. Full versions and site licenses available at a discount from
Classroom Connect.

10. SoftQuad's HoTMetaL. An evaluation copy of the industry leading Web
publishing tool, HoTMetaL PRO. Use this free demo version to quickly and easily
build Web pages for your class or school. Graphical environment interface even
kids can use.

11. Bare Bones Software's BBEdit Lite for Macintosh. An excellent tool to
use when you're building Web pages. A derivative of BBEdit 3.5, the popular and
critically acclaimed text editor for programmers, HTML authors, on-line-service
users, and anyone else who needs to edit plain-text files.

How do I run the CD-ROM on my computer?

This is a hybrid CD-ROM, which means it will work with either an IBM-
compatible PC running Windows 3.1/Windows95 or a Macintosh computer
running System 7.5. We recommend that you have at least 8 megabytes of RAM to
navigate the Internet and use the included software.

To install, simply load the CD-ROM into your CD drive. Then, using any
word-processing program, look for a file called READ ME (on the Mac) or
README.TXT (on a PC). The file contains complete instructions on how to
use this CD-ROM.

TM

✦ A complete online research library.

✦ Deep and broad consumer reference product.

✦ The best way for students and families to do research.

✦ Content is as safe as local public library.

✦ Accessible via the Internet.

✦ Updated daily via satellite.

The way you do research.™

http://www.k12.elibrary.com/classroom

Using The Electric Library, a student can pose a question in plain English and launch a comprehensive and simultaneous search through more than 150 full-text newspapers, over 900 full-text magazines, two international newswires, two thousand classic books, hundreds of maps, thousands of photographs as well as major works of literature and art.

In a matter of seconds, query results are returned to a user ranked in relevancy order, displaying reference data, file size, and grade reading level. With this easy-to-use product a researcher need only click on the document or image of interest and it is automatically downloaded. The materials can also be copied and saved into a word processing document with bibliographic information automatically transferred.

Included in The Electric Library database are materials from world renowned publishers such as Reuters, Simon and Schuster, Gannett, World Almanac, Times Mirror, and Compton's New Media. The Electric Library also incorporates a host of local, ethnic, and special interest publications.

All retrieved information can be downloaded and saved or transferred to a word processor in real time, and used for educational purposes. This includes both the text and images from The Electric Library's databases.

PARTIAL LIST OF ELECTRIC LIBRARY CONTENT

Magazines/Journals
Art Journal
The Economist
Editor & Publisher
Inc.
Lancet
Maclean's
Mother Jones
National review
New Republic
World Press Review

Books/Reference Works
3,000 Great Works of Literature
Monarch Notes
The Complete Works of Shakespeare
The World's Best Poetry
Compton's Encyclopedia
King James Bible
Thematic Dictionary
Webster's Dictionary
World Fact Book

Newspapers/Newswires
Baseball Weekly
Jerusalem Post
La Prensa
Los Angeles Times
Magill's Survey of Cinema
Newsbytes News Service
News India
New York Newsday
Reuters
USA Today

FREE 60-DAY TRIAL!
Offer made in special arrangement with Classroom Connect

PRICING
Individual User: 9^{95} per month
School Site License: $2,000 per year

1-800-638-1639

Infonautics Corporation
900 W. Valley Rd., Suite 1000
Wayne, PA 19087-1830
Voice: 800-304-3542
Fax: 610-971-8859
Email: k12@infonautics.com

Browsing through the Net

Netscape Navigator, Microsoft Internet Explorer, and other Web browsers are fast becoming the all-purpose tool for doing anything on the Internet. Sending email, downloading software, searching gopher menus — ou can do all of it with your Web browser.

Until recently, you needed different programs to do different things on the Internet — an email program to send email, a gopher program to access gopher servers, a newsreader to read Usenet news posts, etc. Your Internet-connected computer probably still has these programs and you may still use them. But you don't have to. Here's why.

When you type a Web site address such as *http://classroom.net* (the Classroom Connect Web site) into your browser, you're actually entering what is called a "Uniform Resource Locator," or URL.

A URL standardizes Internet addresses and the way that Internauts access the various types of online resources. URLs don't have to apply to just Web resources — they can point to gopher databases, newsgroups, ftp sites, and so on.

So how do you get into a gopher site using Netscape, MacWeb, or a browser on a commercial online service such as America Online?

Load your Web software and click the Open URL or Open Location button. Instead of typing *http://* and a corresponding Web address, type *gopher://* or *ftp://* and the address of a gopher or ftp site you'd like to access. Because the formats vary, refer to the accompanying table on page 17 to be sure you follow the appropriate style.

There are many advantages to using a Web browser to access gopher, ftp, and other Internet sites.

- Gopher files and folders, newsgroups and their articles, and ftp directories and files become hyperlinks, so you can use your browser's forward, backward, reload, and other buttons to easily point-and-click your way to information or download files.

- Your browser can give you a clearer picture of where you are when it comes to digging deeper into subdirectories or folders. Notice the Location: window at the top of the ftp.classroom.net screen. It shows the root (ftp.classroom.net) and subdirectory (/wentworth/Internet-Software/IBM/) all at once. If you know the names of subdirectories you need to reach, you can just add them onto the end. Just be sure to separate each subsequent directory name with a slash.

- You can use your browser's bookmark or hotlist feature with any Internet site, thereby incorporating your ftp shortcuts, gopher bookmarks, and favorite Web sites in one convenient location.

- A browser may make it easier to monitor student Internet use, since browsers keep track of sites visited by displaying "followed links" with a different color. Hyperlinks they haven't followed may be blue, while the links they have visited are a different color, usually purple or red.

- Running one browser program instead of three or four separate programs can free up more RAM and hard drive space on your computer, and reduce computer desktop clutter by replacing five or six icons with one.

What about email? Browsers vary in their abilities to incorporate email. In some versions of Netscape (1.1N and below), you can type mailto:user@computer.edu in the Open URL area to send email to someone. Or, you can click on a hyperlinked email address on a Web page and a form pops up that allows you to send a message. But you can't check for new messages and you have few if any customized mailbox, sending and receiving, or filtering options. Netscape 2.0 and newer browsers, such as NetShark and Mariner, however, offer completely integrated email functions similar to popular email programs such as Eudora.